International Labour and Employment Compliance Handbook

www.kluwerlawonline.com

Labour and Employment Compliance in Mexico

International Bar Association

Labour and Employment Compliance in Mexico

Ninth Edition

Oscar De La Vega Gómez

This publication is part of the International Labour and Employment Compliance Handbook, available on www.kluwerlawonline.com

Editors: Salvador del Rey and Robert J. Mignin
Associate Editor: Juan Bonilla

the global voice of
the legal profession

Published by:
Kluwer Law International B.V.
PO Box 316
2400 AH Alphen aan den Rijn
The Netherlands
E-mail: international-sales@wolterskluwer.com
Website: lrus.wolterskluwer.com

Sold and distributed by:
Wolters Kluwer Legal & Regulatory U.S.
7201 McKinney Circle
Frederick, MD 21704
United States of America
E-mail: customer.service@wolterskluwer.com

Printed on acid-free paper.

ISBN 978-94-035-3615-6

e-Book: ISBN 978-94-035-3620-0
web-PDF: ISBN 978-94-035-3621-7

© 2021 Kluwer Law International BV, The Netherlands

All rights reserved. No part of this publication may be reproduced, stored in a retrieval system, or transmitted in any form or by any means, electronic, mechanical, photocopying, recording, or otherwise, without written permission from the publisher.

Permission to use this content must be obtained from the copyright owner. More information can be found at: lrus.wolterskluwer.com/policies/permissions-reprints-and-licensing

Printed in the United Kingdom.

All listed titles are also available on lrus.wolterskluwer.com

1. Argentina: Julio César Stefanoni Zani & Enrique Alfredo Betemps, *Labour and Employment Compliance in Argentina*, 9th edition, 2021 (ISBN 978-94-035-3622-4)
2. Australia: John Tuck, Stephen Price, Rosemary Roach, Jack de Flamingh, Nicholas Ellery & Nick Le Mare, *Labour and Employment Compliance in Australia*, 6th edition, 2021 (ISBN 978-94-035-3914-0)
3. Belgium: Chris Van Olmen, *Labour and Employment Compliance in Belgium*, 6th edition, 2021 (ISBN 978-94-035-3602-6)
4. Brazil: Rodrigo Seizo Takano, Andrea Giamondo Massei & Murilo Caldeira Germiniani, *Labour and Employment Compliance in Brazil*, 8th edition, 2021 (ISBN 978-94-035-3625-5)
5. Canada: Kevin Coon & Adrian Ishak, *Labour and Employment Compliance in Canada*, 2nd edition, 2014 (ISBN 978-90-411-5637-2)
6. Chile: Gerardo Otero A., María Dolores Echeverría F., María de los Ángeles Fernández S. & Javier Sabido, *Labour and Employment Compliance in Chile*, 9th edition, 2021 (ISBN 978-94-035-3635-4)
7. China: King & Wood Mallesons, *Labour and Employment Compliance in China*, 6th edition, 2021 (ISBN 978-94-035-3894-5)
8. France: Pascale Lagesse, *Labour and Employment Compliance in France*, 9th edition, 2021 (ISBN 978-94-035-3672-9)
9. Germany: Gerlind Wisskirchen & Martin Lützeler, *Labour and Employment Compliance in Germany*, 9th edition, 2021 (ISBN 978-94-035-3605-7)
10. India: Manishi Pathak, *Labour and Employment Compliance in India*, 9th edition, 2021 (ISBN 978-94-035-3662-0)
11. Ireland: Duncan Inverarity & Ailbhe Dennehy, *Labour and Employment Compliance in Ireland*, 8th edition, 2021 (ISBN 978-94-035-3911-9)
12. Israel: Pnina Broder-Manor, Helen Raziel & Ilan Winder, *Labour and Employment Compliance in Israel*, 8th edition, 2021 (ISBN 978-94-035-3612-5)
13. Italy: Angelo Zambelli, *Labour and Employment Compliance in Italy*, 9th edition, 2021 (ISBN 978-94-035-3642-2)
14. Japan: Yoshikazu Sugino, *Labour and Employment Compliance in Japan*, 9th edition, 2021 (ISBN 978-94-035-3632-3)
15. Republic of Korea: Sang Wook Cho, Soojung Lee & Christopher Mandel, *Labour and Employment Compliance in the Republic of Korea*, 7th edition, 2021 (ISBN 978-94-035-3645-3)
16. Mexico: Oscar De La Vega Gómez, *Labour and Employment Compliance in Mexico*, 9th edition, 2021 (ISBN 978-94-035-3615-6)
17. The Netherlands: Els de Wind & Cara Pronk, *Labour and Employment Compliance in the Netherlands*, 4th edition, 2018 (ISBN 978-94-035-0470-4)
18. Poland: Barbara Jóźwik, *Labour and Employment Compliance in Poland*, 9th edition, 2021 (ISBN 978-94-035-3675-0)
19. Russia: Anna-Stefaniya Chepik, *Labour and Employment Compliance in Russia*, 2013 (ISBN 978-90-411-4925-1)

20. Saudi Arabia: Sara Khoja & Sarit Thomas, *Labour and Employment Compliance in Saudi Arabia, 4th edition,* 2021 (ISBN 978-94-035-3652-1)
21. South Africa: Susan Stelzner, Stuart Harrison, Brian Patterson & Zahida Ebrahim, *Labour and Employment Compliance in South Africa, 9th edition,* 2021 (ISBN 978-94-035-2773-4)
22. Spain: Salvador del Rey, Ana Campos & Sergi Gálvez Duran, *Labour and Employment Compliance in Spain, 9th edition,* 2021 (978-94-035-3665-1)
23. Turkey: Sertaç Kökenek & Elif Nur Çakır Vurgun, *Labour and Employment Compliance in Turkey, 7th edition,* 2021 (ISBN 978-94-035-3901-0)
24. United Arab Emirates: Sara Khoja & Sarit Thomas, *Labour and Employment Compliance in the United Arab Emirates, 8th edition,* 2021 (ISBN 978-94-035-3655-2)
25. United Kingdom: Ed Mills, Ailie Murray, Anna West, Gareth Walls, Emmie Ellison & Elliot English, *Labour and Employment Compliance in The United Kingdom, 2nd edition,* 2021 (ISBN 978-94-035-3904-1)
26. United States: Andrew J. Boling, Amy de La Lama, William Dugan, Chris Guldberg, Brian Hengesbaugh, Robert J. Mignin, Virginia Mohr, John M. Murphy & Ginger Partee, *Labour and Employment Compliance in the United States, 6th edition,* 2020 (ISBN 978-94-035-2813-7)

International Bar Association
The Global Voice of the Legal Profession

The International Bar Association (IBA), established in 1947, is the world's leading organization of international legal practitioners, bar associations and law societies. The IBA influences the development of international law reform and shapes the future of the legal profession throughout the world. It has a membership of over 40,000 individual lawyers and almost 200 bar associations and law societies spanning all continents. It has considerable expertise in providing assistance to the global legal community.

Grouped into two divisions – the Legal Practice Division and the Public and Professional Interest Division – the IBA covers all practice areas and professional interests, providing members with access to leading experts and up-to-date information. Through the various committees of the divisions, the IBA enables an interchange of information and views among its members as to laws, practices and professional responsibilities relating to the practice of business law around the globe. Additionally, the IBA's high-quality publications and world-class conferences provide unrivalled professional development and network-building opportunities for international legal practitioners and professional associates.

The IBA's Bar Issues Commission provides an invaluable forum for IBA member organisations to discuss all matters relating to law at an international level.

The IBA's Human Rights Institute (IBAHRI) works across the Association, to promote, protect and enforce human rights under a just rule of law, and to preserve the independence of the judiciary and the legal profession worldwide.

Other institutions established by the IBA include the Southern Africa Litigation Centre and the International Legal Assistance Consortium.

Employment and Industrial Relations Law Committee

The aims of the committee are to develop and exchange knowledge of employment and industrial relations law and practice. Members support each other through the provision of innovative ideas and practical assistance on day-to-day issues. In addition, through its journal and through presentations, conferences, the committee ensures the dissemination of up-to-date law and practice in this highly important business area.

International Bar Association Global Employment Institute

The IBA Global Employment Institute (IBA GEI) was formed in early 2010 for the purpose of developing for multinationals and worldwide institutions a global and strategic approach to the key legal issues in the human resources and human capital fields.

Drawing on the resources and expertise of the IBA membership, the IBA GEI will provide a unique contribution in the field of employment, discrimination and immigration law, on a diverse range of global issues, to private and public organizations throughout the world. The IBA GEI is designed to enhance the management, performance and productivity of these organizations and help achieve best practice in their human capital and management functions from a strategic perspective.

The IBA GEI will become the leading voice and authority on global HR issues by virtue of having a number of the world's leading labour and employment practitioners in its ranks, and the support and resource of the world's largest association of international lawyers.

Further information

International Bar Association, 4th Floor, 10 St Bride Street, London EC4A 4AD, United Kingdom, Tel: +44 (0)20 7842 0090, Fax: +44 (0)20 7842 0091, E-mail: member@int-bar.org, www.ibanet.org

About the International Labour and Employment Compliance Handbook

From 1976 through 1988, the International Bar Association and Kluwer Law International published the groundbreaking International Handbook on Contracts of Employment. This Handbook provided one of the first global overviews of the law of the international employment relationship.

Since publishing the first edition, globalization of business has created an increased demand for knowledge of labor and employment laws throughout the world. Therefore, along with Kluwer, we decided to publish an updated Handbook which we have titled the International Labour and Employment Compliance Handbook.

This new Handbook was intended to be a practical guide by providing a general overview of key labor and employment issues in multiple jurisdictions. Each chapter was written so that it is easy to understand by lawyers and non-lawyers alike. Each country author has also followed a standard outline to assist readers in analysing employment issues in each country.

The first edition of this new Handbook included nineteen (19) different countries.

This Handbook would not have been possible without the help and assistance of many people. Most importantly, the individual country authors are all distinguished legal practitioners who spent considerable time drafting and revising their country reports to meet difficult deadlines. We thank each of them. Our friends at Kluwer, especially Ewa Szkatula, have done a wonderful job in keeping the editors and the authors on schedule. Finally, we want to also express our gratitude to Cuatrecasas, Gonçalves Pereira, and Baker & McKenzie LLP for their valuable assistance in the coordination and organization of this project. Our warmest thanks to each of them.

ABOUT THE INTERNATIONAL LABOUR AND EMPLOYMENT COMPLIANCE HANDBOOK

Because of the success of the Handbook, Wolters Kluwer Law & Business decided to publish each country report also as a separate book to give a choice in obtaining the information. We hope this new format will be a helpful and useful resource just like the Handbook. Both formats are available in print and online.

The Editors

Salvador del Rey Guanter
Robert J. Mignin

March 2013

Table of Contents

Author ix

COVID-19 Pandemic xi

Legal Compliance in Mexico 1

1. **Legal Framework: Employment Laws in Mexico** 1
2. **Contracts of Employment** 3
   - 2.1. Overview 3
   - 2.2. Written Employment Contracts 3
   - 2.3. Oral Contracts 5
   - 2.4. Employee Handbooks 6
   - 2.5. Job Description 6
   - 2.6. Offer Letters 7
   - 2.7. Checklist of Dos and Don'ts 7
3. **Recruiting, Interviewing, Screening and Hiring Employees** 8
   - 3.1. Overview 8
   - 3.2. Recruiting 8
   - 3.3. Employment Applications 8
   - 3.4. Pre-employment Enquiries 9
   - 3.5. Pre-employment Tests and Examinations 9
   - 3.6. Background, Reference, and Credit Checks 9
   - 3.7. Interviewing 9
   - 3.8. Hiring Procedures 10
   - 3.9. Fines and Penalties 10
   - 3.10. Checklist of Dos and Don'ts 10
4. **Termination of Employees for Performance or Disciplinary Reasons** 11
   - 4.1. Overview 11
   - 4.2. Separation/Severance Payment 12

		4.3. Fines and Penalties	12
5.	**Managing Performance/Conduct**		13
	5.1.	Overview	13
	5.2.	Coaching and Counselling	13
	5.3.	Written Evaluations	13
	5.4.	Warnings and Suspensions	13
	5.5.	Checklist of Dos and Don'ts	14
	5.6.	Checklist of Dos and Don'ts	14
6.	**Layoffs, Reductions in Force, and/or Redundancies as a Result of Job Eliminations or Other Restructuring**		14
	6.1.	Overview	14
	6.2.	Reductions in Force/Layoffs/Job Eliminations	15
	6.3.	Fines and Penalties	16
	6.4.	Checklist of Dos and Don'ts	16
7.	**Labour and Employment Law Ramifications upon Acquisition or Sale of a Business**		17
	7.1.	Overview	17
	7.2.	Acquisition of a Business (Transfer of Assets)	17
	7.3.	Transfer of Assets Checklist	18
	7.4.	Sale of a Business (No Transfer of Assets)	19
	7.5.	Sale Checklist	19
8.	**Use of Alternative Workforces: Independent Contractors, Contract Employees, and Temporary or Leased Workers**		20
	8.1.	Overview	20
	8.2.	Independent Contractor	20
		8.2.1. Definition	20
		8.2.2. Creating the Relationship	21
		8.2.3. Compensation	21
		8.2.4. Other Terms and Conditions	22
	8.3.	Contract Workers	22
	8.4.	Leased Workers	22
	8.5.	Checklist of Dos and Don'ts	22
9.	**Obligation to Bargain Collectively with Trade Unions: Employees' Right to Strike and a Company's Right to Continue Business Operations**		23
	9.1.	Overview of Unions' Right to Organize	23
	9.2.	Right of Employees to Join Unions	24
	9.3.	How Employees Select Unions	24
	9.4.	Pre-election Campaigning	25
	9.5.	Unfair Labour Practices	25

	9.6.	Relocation of Work/Shutdown of Business	25
	9.7.	Checklist of Dos and Don'ts	26
10.	**Working Conditions: Hours of Work and Payment of Wages: By Statute or Collective Agreements**		**26**
	10.1.	Overview of Wage and Hours Laws	26
	10.2.	Minimum Wage	26
	10.3.	Overtime	27
	10.4.	Meal and Rest Periods	28
	10.5.	Deductions from Wages	28
	10.6.	Garnishment	29
	10.7.	Exemptions to Wage and Hour Laws	29
	10.8.	Child Labour	29
	10.9.	Recordkeeping Requirements	30
		10.9.1. Information That Must Be Maintained	30
		10.9.2. Records That Must Be Retained	31
		10.9.3. Failure to Maintain Required Records	31
	10.10.	Reductions in Compensation Caused by Economic Downtown	31
	10.11.	Checklist of Dos and Don'ts	32
11.	**Other Working Conditions and Benefits: By Statute, Collective Agreements, or Company Policy**		**32**
	11.1.	Health and Other Insurance	32
	11.2.	Pension and Retirement Benefits	33
	11.3.	Vacation and Holiday Payments on Termination	33
	11.4.	Leaves of Absence	34
		11.4.1. Personal Leave	34
		11.4.2. Medical or Sick Leave	34
		11.4.3. Bereavement Leave	35
		11.4.4. Family Leave	35
		11.4.5. Pregnancy Leave	35
		11.4.6. Maternity Leave	35
		11.4.7. Injury at Work	35
	11.5.	Checklist of Dos and Don'ts	37
	11.6.	Telework	37
12.	**Worker's Compensation**		**38**
	12.1.	Overview	38
	12.2.	Checklist of Dos and Don'ts	38
13.	**Company's Obligation to Provide Safe and Healthy Workplace**		**39**
	13.1.	Overview of Safety and Environmental Laws and Regulations	39

	13.2.	Requirements	39
	13.3.	Rights of Employees	40
	13.4.	Rights of Employer	40
	13.5.	Specific Standards	41
	13.6.	Injury or Accident at Work	41
	13.7.	Workplace Violence	42
	13.8.	Fines and Penalties	42
	13.9.	Checklist of Dos and Don'ts	42
14.	**Immigration, Secondment and Foreign Assignment**		43
	14.1.	Overview Laws Controlling Immigration	43
	14.2.	Recruiting, Screening and Hiring Process	43
	14.3.	The Obligation of Employer to Enforce Immigration Laws	43
	14.4.	Fines and Penalties	43
	14.5.	Secondment/Foreign Assignment	44
	14.6.	Checklist of Dos and Don'ts	45
15.	**Restrictive Covenants and Protection of Trade Secrets and Confidential Information**		45
	15.1.	Overview	45
	15.2.	The Law of Trade Secrets	45
	15.3.	Restrictive Covenants and Non-compete Agreements	46
	15.4.	Checklist of Dos and Don'ts	46
16.	**Protection of Whistleblowing Claims**		47
	16.1.	Overview	47
	16.2.	Checklist of Dos and Don'ts	47
17.	**Discrimination in the Workplace**		47
	17.1.	Overview of Anti-discrimination Laws	47
	17.2.	Age Discrimination	48
	17.3.	Race Discrimination	48
	17.4.	Sex Discrimination/Sexual Harassment	48
	17.5.	Handicap and Disability Discrimination	49
	17.6.	National Origin Discrimination	49
	17.7.	Religious Discrimination	50
	17.8.	Military Status Discrimination	50
	17.9.	Pregnancy Discrimination	50
	17.10.	Marital Status Discrimination	51
	17.11.	Sexual Orientation Discrimination	51
	17.12.	Retaliation	51
	17.13.	Constructive Discharge	51
	17.14.	Checklist of Dos and Don'ts	51

18.	**Smoking in the Workplace**	52
	18.1. Overview	52
	18.2. Checklist of Dos and Don'ts	52
19.	**Use of Drugs and Alcohol in the Workplace**	52
	19.1. Overview	52
	19.2. Checklist of Dos and Don'ts	53
20.	**AIDS, HIV, SARS, Blood-Borne Pathogens**	53
	20.1. Overview	53
	20.2. Checklist of Dos and Don'ts	53
21.	**Dress and Grooming Requirements**	54
	21.1. Overview	54
	21.2. Checklist of Dos and Don'ts	54
22.	**Privacy, Technology and Transfer of Personal Data**	54
	22.1. Privacy Rights of Employees	54
	22.2. Checklist of Dos and Don'ts	55
23.	**Workplace Investigations for Complaints of Discrimination, Harassment, Fraud, Theft, and Whistleblowing**	55
	23.1. Overview	55
	23.2. Checklist of Dos and Don'ts	56
24.	**Affirmative Action/Non-discrimination Requirements**	56
	24.1. Overview	56
	24.2. Checklist of Dos and Don'ts	56
25.	**Resolution of Labour, Discrimination and Employment Disputes: Litigation, Arbitration, Mediation and Conciliation**	56
	25.1. Internal Dispute Resolution Process	56
	25.2. Mediation and Conciliation	56
	25.3. Arbitration	57
	25.4. Litigation	57
	25.5. Fines, Penalties and Damages	58
	25.6. Checklist of Dos and Don'ts	58
26.	**Employer Recordkeeping, Data Protection, and Employee Access to Personnel Files and Records**	59
	26.1. Overview	59
	26.2. Personnel Files	59
	26.3. Confidentiality Rules	59
	26.4. Employee Access	59

27. Required Notices and Postings   60
    27.1. Overview   60
    27.2. Checklist of Dos and Don'ts   60

Mexico

AUTHOR

Oscar De la Vega Gómez

Oscar De la Vega Gómez has an LLB/JD, Universidad Iberoamericana, 1983, with Honors and is the founder and managing partner of De La Vega & Martinez Rojas, SC, a leading Firm specialized in labour matters and the sole representative in Mexico of the international alliance L&E Global.

He is a Labour Law Attorney with more than thirty years of experience and leadership in the field. Oscar has focused his practice on labour litigation and counselling, providing legal services to top multinationals. He has specialized in union certification processes, complex collective negotiations and high-profile labour litigations. He also has developed and implemented successful strategies in complex collective matters; and, due to the Labour Reform, he has advised clients on the prevention and management of labour crisis.

He has frequently been a speaker at events organized by national and international associations, such as the International Bar Association (IBA), the Mexican Institute of Executives in Finances (IMEF), the College of Accountants, the National Association of the Chemical Industry (ANIQ), the Maquiladora Industry Council and the Mexican Association in Human Resources Management (AMEDIRH), among others.

He is an active Member of the Human Capital Committee of the Mexican Institute of Finance Executives (IMEF).

Who's Who Legal 2012 recognized Oscar as one of the ten lawyers with the most experience in labour law worldwide, being the only Mexican national on the list, he was included in the list of Latin American Corporate

Counsel Association 2015, he was listed in the Mexican edition of Best Lawyers 2014–2015.

WWL says: 'Top-tier practitioner' Oscar De la Vega Gomez is 'very well known in the market' and is widely regarded as an expert at handling traditional labour law matters.

Acknowledged as the best labour lawyer for 2016 by Who's Who Legal.

Furthermore, he has been recognized as a Recommended Lawyer, Latin American Corporate Counsel Association, 2015; Named, Best Lawyers in Mexico, 2014–2015; Named, Labour and Employment – Chambers Latin America, 2014; Named, International Who's Who of Management Labour and Employment Lawyers – Who's Who Legal, 2012 and 2013.

Oscar has also written several articles which have been published in international publications such as Who's Who Legal, Practical Law Company (PLC), Getting the Deal Through Tax Reform and Its Effects on Social Security, Thomson Reuters, and many others.

ADDRESS

Office Managing Shareholder
Guillermo Gonzalez Camarena 1100, 7th Floor
Col. Santa Fe
Del. Alvaro Obregon, C.P. 01210
Tel.: +52 55.4163.2100 (main)
Tel.: +52 55.4163.2101 (direct)
E-mail: odelavega@dlvmr.com.mx

COVID-19 Pandemic

On 26 March, when the pandemic was quite recent in Mexico, the Department of Labor and Social Welfare, issued a document called 'The Labor Situation in Face of COVID-19, frequent questions' in question 11, the subject document read:

> Can an employer suspend work in a company without a health contingency having been declared?
> Answer: Yes, it can, as long as it continues paying workers their salaries and benefits. In the event of a health contingency decreed by the competent authority, which has not been happened to this date (March 26 2020), the employer will have the obligation of paying the amount of one minimum wage to the workers during the suspension, for up to one month... ."

In regard to this statement, in the sense that the health contingency had not been declared, the World Health Organization (hereinafter 'WHO') had declared the pandemic of the disease caused by the SARS-CoV2 virus (hereinafter 'COVID-19') as a public health international emergency and issued a series of recommendations for its control.

The General Health Council of Mexico, in the decision made on the session held on 19 March 2020, resolved stating that it acknowledged the disease caused by the Sars CoV2 virus in Mexico as a serious disease regarding priority attention and agreed measures for preparation against, prevention and control of the COVID epidemic designed, coordinated and supervised by the Department of Health and implemented by the agencies and entities of the Public Federal Administration (APF), the Legislative and Judicial Powers, the institutions of the National Health System, the governments of the federal states and various organizations of the social and private sectors.

The foregoing meant, without a doubt, that Mexico was facing a health contingency, which was the only thing that could justify the measures taken by the Federal Government, by means of 'stay at home', and by several institutions which had ordered the suspension of work. If we were not in the midst of a health contingency, there would be no legal basis for adopting the measures included in the agreement issued by the Minister of Health, published in the Official Gazette of the Federation on 24 March 2020.

In effect, the measures adopted in Phase 2, which include the so-called social distance, included among others: (1) the suspension of activities in companies and, therefore, the suspension of employment relationships with their employees, (2) the confinement of people in their homes, (3) the restriction to the free transit of people, (4) the suspension of labour for people over 65 years of age and other groups considered to be vulnerable; among many other measures, including the possibility of imposing penalizations and the using public force to enforce these measures. The agreement was sanctioned by the President of the Republic, under the terms of the decree published in the Official Gazette of the Federation, also on 24 March 2020.

It was clear that measures to prevent and fight the health contingency were being implemented; nevertheless, the labour authority contended that the contingency had not been declared, with the sole purpose of circumventing the legal provisions of the Federal Labour Law, as explained below.

The institution of collective suspension of work exists in our Labour Law. Its objective being to avoid the termination of employment relationships by just suspending them in face of extraordinary situations that affect the normal development of activities in the workplace, allowing the employer to preserve the viability of the company by reducing labour costs during the contingency and ensuring a compensation that allows the worker to face this extraordinary situation, as long as the work suspension implies: the non-provision of the service and, therefore, the non-causation of the salary. This institution is provided for in Article 427 of the Federal Labour Law and reads as it follows:

> Article 427......
> (...)
> The suspension of labor or work, declare by the competent health authority in case of a health contingency.

It is important to highlight that when this article refers to 'declare', it does so in relation to the 'work', not to the contingency: therefore, the suspension of work is declared due to the contingency, the contingency is not the one being declared. Notwithstanding the aforementioned, when different authorities were facing the labour consequences of the health contingency, it was contended that the emergency had not been declared, as if the 'declaration' were a legal formality required by law, but this requirement does not exist either in the Constitution or in the General Law on Health. In the absence of a contingency (whether the word 'declaration' is used or not), the measures that have been ordered would have no basis: the suspension of activities in companies, the confinement of people in their homes, the limitation of the free transit of people, to name some of them.

This reasoning of the authorities had no other purpose than making the articles that regulate the suspension of work by reason of a health contingency unenforceable and concluding that there is no regulation in place in the Federal Labour Law to solve the situation.

Then, on 30 March, in a meeting of the General Health Council a 'Health emergency due to force majeure was declared'. Although this declaration made created confusion between employers, it more or less invalidated the scope of the aforementioned provision and forced employers to invoke another subsection of said article as the motive for a suspension caused by force majeure, with very different effects, as the compensation paid to the workers according to this last fraction consists of one month of full salary and, not the one minimum wage for up to one month that would have applied if the suspension of labour relationships was due to the suspension of work.

Then, on 30 March 2020, it was published in the Official Gazette of the Federation, a decree declaring the immediate suspension of work from 30 March to 30 April 2020 on activities that are not essential within the public, private and social sectors, with the objective of mitigating the spread and transmission of the SARS-CoV-2 virus. This suspension of activities was continuously extended and, with certain modifications, it is still in force up until today.

On the downside, as it can be understood from the above, the coronavirus pandemic created a new set of challenges for all companies, as the actions taken by the government created a great amount of economic and legal uncertainty within the companies. Many businesses considered as non-essential stopped activities for a long period of time and that generated economic losses to these companies, which, in many occasions, led to the termination of numerous employees and/or the company's shut down. However, the pandemic also generated the opportunity for companies to reinvent the way they do business, especially with regards to giving the opportunity for employees to work remotely. As a result, different amendments to the Federal Labour Law were done, including one published in the Official Gazette of the Federation on 11 January 2021 regarding, 'Home-Office'.

Legal Compliance in Mexico

1. LEGAL FRAMEWORK: EMPLOYMENT LAWS IN MEXICO

The Mexican legal system is one based on the civil law tradition, which is a highly systematized and codified system of law. Thus, in Mexican law, the main sources of law are codified texts that derive from the provisions of the Mexican Constitution.[1] As the utmost source of law in Mexico, the Constitution has specific provisions set forth to protect the rights of man and citizen. These rights, previously referred to as individual guarantees in the civil tradition (constitutional rights) and now regulated as human rights, are classified in relation to the rights they safeguard: (i) constitutional rights of equality; (ii) constitutional rights of freedom; (iii) constitutional rights of due process of law (or legal certainty); and (iv) constitutional social rights – which by definition are those that were created with the intention to protect the common interests of a specific group as a collectivity (e.g., workers, students, common land farmers). The applicable legislations for labour law in Mexico derive from the constitutional provisions on social rights for workers in Article 123.

Furthermore, Article 123 of the Mexican Constitution provides protection for the collective interests of workers by establishing general employee rights that seek a balance in the employer–employee relationship, including but not limited to the following:

(a) setting the maximum limit of working hours per week;
(b) equality rights;
(c) weekly rest days;

---

1. 'Political Constitution of the United States of Mexico'. [*Constitución Política de los Estados Unidos Mexicanos.*] Published on the Federal Official Gazette on 5 Feb. 1917. Last amendment published on 24 Feb. 2017 on the Federal Official Gazette.

(d) mandatory rest days in the year (holidays or long weekends);
(e) employees' right to profit-sharing;
(f) maternity leave;
(g) limitations on the work of minors;
(h) limitations on work of pregnant and breastfeeding mothers;
(i) paid vacation periods;
(j) right to unionize, to strike and lockout, and right to collective bargaining;
(k) minimum salaries;
(l) limitations on work shifts;
(m) overtime;
(n) social security rights (such as the establishment of a housing fund for workers);
(o) Christmas bonus;
(p) mandatory training;
(q) labour authorities (competence and jurisdiction), among others.

Furthermore, the following Mexican laws govern all labour relationships in Mexico, regardless of whether or not the workers are Mexican citizens:

- Federal Labour Law (FLL), 1970.
- Social Security Law (SSL), 1995.
- National Workers Housing Fund Institute's Law, 1972.

FLL is the most important employment legislation in Mexico. It defines a 'labour relationship'[2] as the rendering of a subordinated personal service by one person to another, in exchange for a wage.

The main element of any labour relationship is *subordination*,[3] which the Mexican Federal Supreme Court has defined as the employer's legal right to control and direct the employee and the employee's duty to obey the employer.[4] Once a labour relationship exists, the rights and obligations provided for by the FLL automatically enter into legal force, regardless of how the agreement is defined by the parties.

Additionally, the SSL is the legislation that contains the stipulations intended to provide further social benefits for the collectivity, specifically aimed for the employers and the employees. The SSL covers the various rights and duties of both employee and employer with respect to retirement funds and healthcare benefits provided for by the authorities.

---

2. Article 22. Federal Labor Law (FLL). [*Ley Federal del Trabajo.*] Published on the Federal Official Gazette on 1 Apr. 1970. Last amendment published on 12 Jun. 2015 on the Federal Official Gazette.
3. Article 134, para. III. FLL.
4. 'Duty of Obedience of Employee to Employer. Limits Of'. Registry No. 273866. *Mexican Jurisprudence – Isolated Theses*. Sixth Epoch. Fourth Chamber. Weekly Federal Court Report. Fifth Part, LXXXIII., 16. Labour Law.

The National Workers Housing Fund Institute's Law was created with the purpose of providing support for the employees in order to acquire their own homes. A National Housing Fund was created for employees in order for them to have access to a government-run mortgage (credit institution) and acquire their own homes. There is an obligation from the employer to deposit the corresponding portion of the employees' salary to the National Housing Fund in order for the employee to qualify for the mortgage option (among others).

2. CONTRACTS OF EMPLOYMENT

2.1. OVERVIEW

Written employment agreements in Mexico are mandatory. Every employee must enter into an individual employment agreement with the employer and set out the terms and conditions of the employment in Mexico, there's no 'employment-at-will'. An employer must have justified cause (as defined by the FLL) in order to terminate the employment relationship; if not, the employer must compensate the unjustly terminated employee accordingly (FLL stipulates the amount for severance payments). Notwithstanding the previous statement, in the given case that an employment relationship exists and there is no written agreement, the employee's constitutional and statutory rights are not waived or affected by this omission.

In the case of Unions, there is an additional agreement that is negotiated and entered into by the Union and the employer in order to promote the creation or improvement of the labour conditions for the employees as a collectivity, and in turn, the employer obtains a loyal and solid workforce. The Collective Bargaining Agreement (hereinafter 'CBA') is renewable and cannot contain provisions that stipulate the waiver of the basic constitutional and statutory rights or benefits for the employees as a collectivity. It can always be more favourable than the constitutional and statutory requirements but never less than the latter.

2.2. WRITTEN EMPLOYMENT CONTRACTS

Article 24 of the FLL provides that working conditions must be established in writing, and each party must be provided with a copy of the employment agreement. In addition, Article 25 states that the individual employment agreement must contain the following information:

(i) Name, nationality, age, sex, civil status, Unique Population Registry Code [*Clave Única de Registro de Población (CURP)*], Tax ID number, and domicile of the employee and the employer, if applicable.
(ii) Whether the employment is for a specific job or term, initial training, permanent, and if it is subject to a probationary period.
(iii) The service or services to be provided, as specifically as possible (*job description*).
(iv) The place or places where the employee will work.
(v) The work schedules.
(vi) Amount of salary and any fringe benefits.
(vii) Date and place where the salary is to be paid.
(viii) An indication that the employee will be trained according to the plans and programmes established by the employer.
(ix) Amount of rest and vacation days and any other conditions agreed to by the employee and the employer.
(x) The employee's beneficiaries who will receive the outstanding benefits and seniority premium in case the employee dies during the employment relationship or in case of disappearance derived from a criminal act.

Every employment agreement contains an implied relationship of mutual trust and confidence. Furthermore, employment agreements cannot contain an employee's acceptance to waive the necessary legal grounds for justified dismissal on the part of the employer and the following minimum benefits:

(a) *Social Security Benefits.* All employees must be registered with and contribute to the:
  (i) Mexican Institute of Social Security [*Instituto Mexicano del Seguro Social (IMSS)*].
  (ii) National Workers Housing Fund Institute.
  (iii) Retirement Savings Programme.
  (iv) National Fund Institute for Workers' Consumption [*Instituto del Fondo Nacional para el Consumo de los Trabajadores (INFONACOT)*], which is a governmental institution that provides financial aid to employees for the acquisition of goods and services. This is mandatory as of 1 December 2013.
(b) *Profit-Sharing.* Employees are entitled to share in the employer's profits, currently fixed at 10% of the company's gross, pre-tax income.
(c) *Paid Mandatory Holidays.* The FLL requires that employees be paid for government holidays.
(d) *Vacation Premium.* Employees are paid an extra 25% of the salary to which they are entitled during their vacation period.

(e) *Christmas Bonus.* Employees have the right to a bonus of at least fifteen days of their daily base salary, which must be paid by no later than 20th December of each year.

CBAs must also be in writing and contain the following information:

(1) names and domiciles of the parties executing the CBA;
(2) the address of the facilities where the CBA will be applicable;
(3) duration or whether it is for an indefinite term or specific job;
(4) work schedules;
(5) rest days and holidays;
(6) salary amounts;
(7) employee training;
(8) initial training for new hires;
(9) integration and operation of the employee–employer committees as established by law;
(10) other conditions agreed upon by the parties.

CBAs must be filed in the Local or Federal Conciliation and Arbitration Board, depending on competence and jurisdiction. Competence and jurisdiction of the Conciliation and Arbitration Boards are determined by the employer's main business activities in accordance with the applicable FLL provisions.

Please note that, on 1 May 2019, an important amendment to the FLL was enacted and, due to this reform, the Federal Centre of Conciliation and Labour Registration was created and has started to take the registration function of the Conciliation and Arbitration Board. This Centre's aim is to centralize the registration of all CBAs in the country, regardless of the main business activity of the employer, meaning that all CBAs will be part of the federal jurisdiction.

2.3. ORAL CONTRACTS

Oral employment agreements are not expressly regulated by the FLL since written employment agreements are mandatory under the said legislation. However, the FLL stipulates that the lack of a written agreement does not prevent employees from exercising their constitutional and statutory rights. The absence of a written agreement represents a fault on the part of the employer.

2.4. EMPLOYEE HANDBOOKS

Employee handbooks per se are not regulated by the FLL; however, each company or business may establish Internal Labour Regulations (hereinafter 'ILR'), defined by the FLL in its Chapter V (Articles 422–425), as a set of mandatory provisions applicable to both employees and employers in connection with the activities to be performed in a business or company (the ILR could be interpreted as a form of 'handbook'). In accordance with FLL Article 424, the conditions of the ILR will be expressly agreed upon by a joint commission comprised of an equal number of representatives of the employees and the employer. Subsequently, the ILR must be filed before the competent Conciliation and Arbitration Board or, if applicable, before the Federal Centre of Conciliation and Labour Registration in order to be enforceable. The ILR will be mandatory for both employer and employees as of the date on which they are filed before the corresponding authority.

The ILR must establish the guidelines with respect to:

(1) employee work schedules, lunch, and breaks;
(2) days and times for the cleaning of facilities, machinery, equipment and tools;
(3) time and place for salary payments;
(4) measures to be taken in order to prevent work accidents, and first-aid training;
(5) time and procedures for employee medical exams, prior to and during employment with the company;
(6) requirements to obtain permits and/or leaves of absence;
(7) disciplinary actions and the application thereof; and
(8) in general, any and all other necessary company standards agreed upon between the parties of the ILR commission.

Sufficient copies of the ILR should be made and distributed between all employees. An employer should also make sure the ILR are posted on highly visible areas of the company so that all parties involved are fully aware of their rights/duties in the company.

2.5. JOB DESCRIPTION

As mentioned in section 2.2 above, Article 25 fraction III of the FLL states that the employment agreement shall describe as specifically as possible the service or services to be provided by the employee, which is understood as the job description requirement.

To this respect, the employer has an obligation to state, in as much detail as possible, an accurate description of what service or services are expected from the employee in the employment agreement. This provision is intended to provide protection for both employer and employee by determining employee obligations to perform while under the employer's service. An example of the importance of the detailed job descriptions can be seen in employees whose work requires extensive travelling. For this particular matter, an employer must make sure that the job description includes an express agreement on the part of the employee to travel in order to correctly fulfil the employment obligations and conditions.

2.6. OFFER LETTERS

Offer letters are not regulated in the FLL; however, in practice, they are very common. When an offer letter is not subsequently replaced by an individual employment agreement, it is considered binding on the parties. It could be enforceable even if the prospected employer revokes the offer before employment starts, due to the general principle of labour law that states that it is vital to promote employment certainty in employees.

2.7. CHECKLIST OF DOS AND DON'TS

- Do draft employment agreements pursuant to Articles 24 and 25 of the FLL.
- Do document and regulate sales incentives and/or commissions programmes.
- Do bear in mind that labour relations in Mexico are bilateral, and it is not possible for the employer to modify any work conditions without employee consent.
- Do include a detailed job description in the employment agreement.
- Do include a term in any offer letter for the job applicant to accept the offer.
- Do not hire expatriates without properly documenting the labour relation with the Mexican subsidiary.
- Do not forget that in Mexico there is no 'employment-at-will'.

3. RECRUITING, INTERVIEWING, SCREENING AND HIRING EMPLOYEES

3.1. OVERVIEW

In general terms, the employer has the freedom to ask the questions it considers convenient to a candidate in all phases of the recruitment process; in other words, there is almost no limitation to the scope of such questions from a legal standpoint. However, company policy and international guidelines might require global corporations to adhere to stricter procedures in the recruitment, interview and screening processes.

3.2. RECRUITING

Given that there are no specific laws or rules applicable to recruitment, employers may, in their own judgment or interests or in accordance with company policy and interests, determine all necessary requirements for employment.

Laws regulating discrimination are not extensively developed in Mexico, but the Federal Law to Prevent and Avoid Discrimination and the FLL state that workers shall not be discriminated against on the grounds of race, nationality, sex, age, disability, religion, political opinion, migratory condition, health, sexual preferences, or social rank. Even though the FLL prohibits discrimination, in practice there is, unfortunately, no action against employer discrimination.

3.3. EMPLOYMENT APPLICATIONS

On the employment application, employers can request information from an applicant regarding his/her socioeconomic data, educational background, prior employment, drug screening, medical conditions, family situation. Criminal background screening is considered discriminatory and is no longer permitted, with limited exceptions such as certain positions in banking and financial sector.

Notwithstanding the above, it is advisable to include a specific provision in the application form whereby the applicant acknowledges and agrees to the background check, and the employer attests that the information provided will be kept confidential. Employers shall also be mindful of compliance with data privacy law and regulations.

3.4. PRE-EMPLOYMENT ENQUIRIES

As mentioned previously, employers have great flexibility regarding the information that may be gathered about applicants except pregnancy status for working women or any other information that may imply a discriminatory practice.

3.5. PRE-EMPLOYMENT TESTS AND EXAMINATIONS

Drug screening and pre-employment physicals for applicants are generally permitted, with the applicant's consent. Additionally, the results of tests and information provided in interviews must be kept confidential and in accordance with the privacy notice delivered to the employee or applicant.

Employers may make enquiries regarding the consumption of alcohol or tobacco without restrictions.

3.6. BACKGROUND, REFERENCE, AND CREDIT CHECKS

Letters of recommendation are usually required by employers. Background and reference checks are generally allowed but are subject to the applicant's consent; the law is silent to this particular respect, but it is recommended that employer secures applicant's consent. The information obtained has to be handled in a confidential manner and in accordance with the privacy notice delivered to the employee or applicant.

Credit checks are mandatory only for certain executive positions in the banking and finance sectors, but not for other positions or other industries; therefore, denying a job due to bad credit history may be considered as discriminatory.

The FLL allows employers to terminate any employee, without any further liability to the employer, within thirty days following the employee's first day on the job or hiring date, if the employee used false documentation or false references to obtain employment, or deceives the employer about qualifications that he/she does not have.

3.7. INTERVIEWING

The employer has the freedom to ask any questions in any phase of the recruitment process. There is no real limit set by law as to the pertinence of the questions allowed; however, common sense is applied under these circumstances. During interviews, employers may ask for and corroborate any financial information, educational or employment information, drug screen results, medical condition, family situation and criminal history.

3.8. Hiring Procedures

The FLL does not provide for any special hiring process; therefore, employers do not have to follow any specific guidelines, unless agreed with the Union in the CBA (such as hiring only union members). However, depending on the position, normal practice dictates that all possible employees must first fill out an employment application, whereby all those interested in working for a company provide certain information, such as personal information, academic background, references, qualifications, skills and job experience.

A second phase involves an interview with the applicant and, for some companies, work history and economic background checks, directly or through third parties.

Since the company will gather personal data of the applicant, employers are also required to deliver a privacy notice to the same, in order to comply with the Federal Law for the Protection of Personal Data in the Possession of Private Parties (FLPPD).

3.9. Fines and Penalties

As the recruiting and hiring process is not regulated, the only fine that can be incurred by the employer during this process is in case the employer requires a medical certificate that demonstrates that the applicant is NOT pregnant in order to hire, promote or keep her job. Additionally, the employer could incur unwanted negative publicity if it requests information regarding sexual orientation, pregnancy or any other information that could be construed as discriminatory.

3.10. Checklist of Dos and Don'ts

- Do set forth the necessary requirements for employment.
- Do request information regarding personal information, background, references, skills, qualifications and experience.
- Do request educational, financial, family, medical and employment information.
- Do perform background checks.

- Do request an applicant's consent before performing medical examinations and drug screenings.
- Do not disclose the results of medical examinations or drug screenings.
- Do not make enquiries regarding sexual orientation.
- Do not make enquiries or request information about pregnancy.
- Verify and corroborate all information provided by applicants during the hiring process.

Do provide applicants with a privacy notice.

4. TERMINATION OF EMPLOYEES FOR PERFORMANCE OR DISCIPLINARY REASONS

4.1. OVERVIEW

Employee termination is only possible if the employer has a justifiable cause. Article 47 of the FLL specifies that the following conducts are cause for dismissal:

(1) if the employee, or the union that proposed or recommended the employee, deceives the employer with false certificates or references that certify that the employee has certain abilities, skills or qualities which he or she does not have;
(2) dishonest or violent behaviour against the employer, customers and/or providers, while on the job;
(3) dishonest or violent behaviour against co-workers that disrupts work discipline;
(4) threatening, insulting, or abusing the employer or the employer's family, unless provoked or acting in self-defence;
(5) intentionally damaging company property;
(6) negligently causing serious damage to company property;
(7) carelessly threatening workplace safety;
(8) immoral behaviour, sexual harassment and bullying in the workplace;
(9) disclosure of trade secrets or confidential information;
(10) more than three unjustified absences in a thirty-day period;
(11) disobeying the employer without justification;
(12) failure to follow safety procedures;
(13) reporting to work under the influence of alcohol or non-prescription drugs;
(14) a prison sentence;
(15) lack of necessary documents or permissions in order to provide the service; or
(16) any other similar acts.

In view of the foregoing, it is clear that poor performance is not a justifiable cause for termination.

4.2. SEPARATION/SEVERANCE PAYMENT

Termination payment is calculated depending upon the cause of termination:

- *Voluntary resignation:* The employer must pay all due benefits, including sales incentives, on a prorated basis up to the termination date. If the employee has at least fifteen years of seniority, he or she is also entitled to a seniority premium of twelve days' salary for each year of service capped to twice the minimum daily salary in force (the current general minimum wage is of MXN 141.7, which is equal to USD 7.03).
- *Termination with a cause:* The employer has to pay all due benefits, including commissions, on a prorated basis until the date of termination, and the seniority premium of twelve days of salary for each year of service (with a cap of twice the minimum daily salary in the same terms as explained before).
- *Termination without cause:* Employees that are terminated without cause are entitled to the following lump sum severance: (1) three months of the employee's daily aggregate salary, plus; (2) twenty days of the employee's daily aggregate salary for each year of service; (3) a seniority premium of twelve days salary for each year of service (with a cap of twice the minimum daily salary in the same terms as explained before); (4) due benefits.

4.3. FINES AND PENALTIES

There are no fines or penalties regarding this matter, except severance payments described above in case there is no justified cause for termination. If an employee who was unjustifiably terminated has been duly compensated according to FLL requirements, there is no real need to bring a lawsuit against the employer unless the employee wishes to be reinstated for which the employee will refuse to accept payment and request reinstatement in his lawsuit.

5. MANAGING PERFORMANCE/CONDUCT

5.1. Overview

The FLL does not provide any regulations on the evaluation or discipline of employees. In order for performance and conduct rules to be enforceable, they have to be included in the ILRs, performance agreements, codes of conduct, internal policies and/or individual or collective employment agreements. Employers and employees agree upon what constitutes misconduct and the resulting penalties, or the performance targets and the consequences on the lack of performance thereof on the part of the employee.

5.2. Coaching and Counselling

The FLL does not require employers to provide coaching or counselling. Therefore, employers can determine their own policies and procedures. Since labour relations in Mexico are bilateral, the employee or the union must agree to these policies and procedures.

5.3. Written Evaluations

It is quite common for employers to perform written evaluations of their employees. Such evaluations are useful not only to evaluate employee performance but also to decide on wage increases, performance improvement plans and, in some cases, possible termination of employment.

Performance per se is not considered a legal cause for termination without liability to the employer (*see* section 4.1 above).

5.4. Warnings and Suspensions

The FLL states that any penalty imposed on an employee must be included in the company's ILRs. They could consist of a written or verbal warning, suspension, or even termination with no liability to the employer. There are no provisions on the FLL for a specific process of warnings and suspensions; these processes are agreed upon on the ILR. Justified termination as a consequence of an infraction has to be in accordance with Article 47 of the FLL.

Suspensions shall not exceed eight days and must necessarily be included in the ILR.

5.5. CHECKLIST OF DOS AND DON'TS

– Do have ILR that regulates the conduct and performance of work within the company.
– Do penalize employees who violate the company's ILR.
– Do perform written evaluations on employees.
– Do not suspend any employee for more than eight days.
– Do not dismiss an employee based on poor performance, except in the case of salespersons and/or if you have enough hard evidence to prove such poor performance during a trial.

5.6. CHECKLIST OF DOS AND DON'TS

– Do dismiss an employee if there is a justifiable cause and follow the procedure established by the FLL.
– Do not dismiss an employee if there is not a justified cause, or otherwise be prepared to pay the legal severance and execute a termination agreement.
– Do ratify termination agreements with the Labour Conciliation and Arbitration Board, or, if applicable before the Conciliation Centres or Courts.

6. LAYOFFS, REDUCTIONS IN FORCE, AND/OR REDUNDANCIES AS A RESULT OF JOB ELIMINATIONS OR OTHER RESTRUCTURING

6.1. OVERVIEW

According to the FLL, there must be a legally permitted cause of termination that substantiates the collective dismissal. The severance payment and the subsequent procedure will be determined depending on the cause.

The first step is to determine whether the company has unionized workers and confidential employees. If it does, the working conditions of the union workers are governed by the CBA. Therefore, both the termination of the union workers and the CBA must be negotiated with the Union.

Concerning the termination of individual employment relations with union workers, the FLL sets forth a formula to calculate the amount of severance to be paid to each employee, as described above in section 4.2.

The aggregate salary of union workers must include: (1) the base salary; (2) any other benefit in cash or in kind (such as life insurance, savings fund, food coupons, vacation premium, year-end bonus); and (3) any other benefit provided to the employee for services rendered.

In practice, some labour unions claim the payment of a four-month indemnity plus twenty days of aggregate daily salary for each year of services rendered, arguing that the termination of the employment relationship is a consequence of the implementation of new working procedures by the parent company. In other cases, the union claims an additional premium for the closing of industrial operations that may represent an additional percentage to the indemnity contemplated by law.

The employer also has an obligation to pay a seniority premium to each employee being terminated. This premium is equal to twelve days of salary for each year of service rendered, with a cap at the equivalent of two times the minimum daily salary. Mandatory fringe benefits must be paid in arrears at the time of termination.

Upon conclusion of the negotiations, an agreement will be filed before the Local Conciliation and Arbitration Board, or the Federal Centre of Conciliation and Labour Registration, or Courts when applicable or for the liquidation of all union workers. The above will enable the employer to freely dispose of its real estate and goods (machinery, raw materials, buildings, etc.).

Additionally, it is a common practice to liquidate confidential employees using the same basis as for the union workers. In some cases, those who actively participate in the closing operations will receive a 'stay-on' bonus.

6.2. REDUCTIONS IN FORCE/LAYOFFS/JOB ELIMINATIONS

A *collective redundancy* takes place if the company either:

– permanently ceases to operate; or
– permanently closes a department or specific area of the business, leading to a reduction of personnel in that area or department.

In these circumstances, the employer must negotiate with trade unions if it wishes to make employees who belong to these unions redundant or introduce any amendments to the CBA. Once negotiations have taken place, an agreement must be signed and registered with the Labour Board before terminating the employment contracts. The CBA must also be terminated so that the employer can freely dispose of its real estate and goods.

If employees who belong to trade unions are made redundant, they are entitled to a severance payment as above described in section 4.2.

In cases where employees are made redundant due to a modernization plan (e.g., installation of new machinery or adoption of new production processes), they are entitled to compensation equal to four months daily aggregate salary in one single payment and twenty days daily aggregate salary for every year worked in the company. Unions sometimes demand extra compensation to be paid. In addition, employees who belong to a trade union, as well as management employees who do not belong to a union, receive their salary and fringe benefits up until the date on which their contracts are terminated.

As provided by Article 434 of the FLL, the following grounds can represent a legal basis for collective redundancy:

- Force majeure not attributable to the employer, in which case written notice must be given to the Labour Board.
- Inability to operate at a profit, in which case prior approval from the Labour Board is required.
- Depletion of the natural resources in an industry such as mining, in which case prior approval from the Labour Board is required.
- Permanent depletion of the minerals in a mine.
- Bankruptcy resulting in the permanent closure of the company or reduction in its operations, in which case prior approval from the Labour Board is required.

In all cases (except the depletion of minerals in a mine), employees are entitled to severance pay equivalent to three months aggregate daily salary and to a seniority premium based on their years of service.

It is important to mention that if the collective dismissal only represents a reduction of workforce in a facility or company, then the employees with less seniority shall be dismissed first. The CBA may establish additional procedures or classes of protected employees.

6.3. FINES AND PENALTIES

There are no fines or penalties established by the law for employers; however, the employees may challenge the dismissal with the Labour Board, asking for either the reinstatement in their previous job or a severance payment.

6.4. CHECKLIST OF DOS AND DON'TS

- Do pay the respective severance payment in the case of dismissal without cause.
- Do negotiate with trade unions for redundancies.
- Do execute and file termination agreements with the Conciliation and Arbitration Board or, if applicable before Conciliation Centres or Courts.

MEXICO

7. LABOUR AND EMPLOYMENT LAW RAMIFICATIONS UPON ACQUISITION OR SALE OF A BUSINESS

7.1. Overview

Employment obligations arising from an acquisition or sale of a business will depend on the type and amount of assets being transferred.

In Mexico, there are essentially three ways of dealing with employees upon the acquisition of a going concern (resulting from a transfer of assets essential for operations in the sense that they are necessary in order to keep the plant running):

(1) the seller can terminate the employment relationship with its employees and pay them the severance payment required by law;
(2) the buyer can acquire the employees along with the rest of the business by way of an 'employer substitution'; or
(3) a combination of the two can be implemented.

Article 41 of the FLL establishes the legal figure of employer substitution, where the employment relationship shall not be affected, due to the acquisition or sale of the company; therefore, the existing legal relationship does not change, and the substitute acquires the obligations and rights of the person being substituted.

The Third Collegiate Labour Court of the First Circuit (which corresponds to Mexico City) has determined that there is employer substitution whenever an operation meets the following core elements: (1) the transfer of assets from one company or legal entity to another; (2) the use of the same tools or assets with which the substituted employer operated; (3) the formation of the new company under the same commercial business; and (4) the use of the same work centre and its uninterrupted use.

Furthermore, a recent amendment to the Federal Labour Law has added a third paragraph to Article 41 and established that, in order for an employer substitution to be valid, the assets of the substituted company or establishment have to be transferred to the substitute employer.

7.2. Acquisition of a Business (Transfer of Assets)

According to the FLL and to the SSL, when the assets of a company are transferred, *employer substitution* will arise. Specifically, under Article 41 of the FLL, the original employment relationship continues with the new employer; and the period of service for the former employer is added to the length of service for the new employer. The new employer will have to comply with all employment conditions and grant the same benefits given by the former employer to the employees.

Employees do not have to consent to the substitution because it operates as a matter of law; however, it is a legal obligation to deliver a written notice to each employee and the social security agencies regarding the employer substitution.

The FLL states that the new employer will be jointly liable for the obligations assumed by the former employer (including any unpaid social security dues), and such liability shall last for: (i) six months beginning on the date the employees and/or the union were given notice of the employer substitution; and (ii) six months for any unpaid social security dues. In light of an employer substitution, the employment conditions cannot be modified. The previous employment relationship continues, and the new employer is jointly liable with the former employer for a period of up to six months.

After the expiration of this six-month term, the new employer becomes the sole party responsible for said obligations. The above-mentioned terms for joint liability will run from the date employees are notified of the employer substitution.

It is important to bear in mind that an employer substitution does not require the consent of the Union or the employees because it operates as a matter of law; therefore, the process is carried out by written notification to the employees and social security agencies.

7.3. Transfer of Assets Checklist

- Coordinate strategy of sale/acquisition between the parties.
- Prepare the 'essential assets' inventory that the company will transfer to the new company as part of the employer substitution.
- Verify that the legal definition of 'essential assets' 1 complies with the appropriate tax laws.
- Prepare a service agreement to be executed by and between the companies.
- Prepare and deliver the notice to be given to the employees and/or the Union.
- Discuss an employer substitution with the Union and coordinate the delivery of the substitution agreement to the Conciliation and Arbitration Board.
- Prepare the paperwork in order to carry out the employer substitution with the IMSS and the Mexican Workers Housing Fund Institute (*Instituto Nacional del Fondo para la Vivienda de los Trabajadores (INFONAVIT)*).
- Deliver the substitution notice to employees, tax, immigration and labour authorities.

7.4. Sale of a Business (No Transfer of Assets)

If there is not a transfer of assets, then there would be no employer substitution. In this case, there are two alternatives to transfer employees.

The first alternative is for the 'old' company could terminate the employment agreements and hire them again on the 'new' company. If the seniority of the employees is recognized by the new employer, no severance would be paid. The employees would receive the payment of their due benefits and salary from the former employer.

The second alternative is to terminate the employment agreements without acknowledging the employees' seniority. The former employer would have to pay severance consisting of:

- three months aggregate daily salary; plus
- twenty days aggregate daily salary per each year of service; plus
- the corresponding seniority premium (capped at twice the minimum daily wage in force).

In this case, the employees would also receive the payment of their benefits and salary as of their transfer date.

In any of the above-mentioned alternatives, a release is signed by the employee in favour of the former employer and the new employer assumes no liability for those services rendered prior to the signing of such release. Also, the new employer is entitled to establish new working conditions.

7.5. Sale Checklist

- Coordinate strategy to transfer the employees.
- Determine whether or not the new employer will recognize employee seniority. Execute termination agreements between each employee and the former employer, which should be ratified with the Conciliation and Arbitration Board, or if applicable, Conciliation Centres or Courts. However, if done privately it is recommended to do it before a Public Notary.
- Determine new working conditions to prepare new employment agreements for employees.
- Discuss and negotiate the transfer with the Union to avoid potential calls to strike.

8. USE OF ALTERNATIVE WORKFORCES: INDEPENDENT CONTRACTORS, CONTRACT EMPLOYEES, AND TEMPORARY OR LEASED WORKERS

8.1. Overview

It is quite common in Mexico to use alternative workforces. In principle, all company activities can be outsourced unless the CBA establishes that certain activities must be performed by union workers.

When entering into outsourcing or independent contractor agreements, the company must bear in mind that pursuant to the FLL, the existence of an employment relationship is presumed between a person who performs a service and a person who receives the service, in return for payment or compensation. The FLL further establishes that an employment relationship means (regardless of the act from which it originates) the performance of work under the authority of another person, in return for compensation. The Supreme Court has provided that the essential element in an employment relationship is subordination, which is understood as the legal authority of the employer to command the obedience of a person who renders services on its behalf.

In view of the above, the existence of a subordinate relationship will determine the real nature of the relationship between the individuals rendering the services and the beneficiary.

8.2. Independent Contractor

8.2.1. Definition

There is no legal definition of independent contractor; however, such status depends primarily on whether a subordinated relationship among the parties exists; that is, if the individual is subordinated to the beneficiary of the services, then an employment relationship will be deemed to exist, regardless of the contract that is executed by and between the parties.

Due to the foregoing, hiring independent contractors in Mexico carries risks as labour, social security and tax authorities may find that such a relationship is of a labour nature rather than a civil relationship.

A subordinate relationship exists if the individual rendering services are under company control, if the company has the authority to set his work schedule, the place where his services will be rendered, those to whom he must report to, the time over which services are to be provided or the continuity or regularity of the services provided.

8.2.2. Creating the Relationship

Pursuant to the FLL, the existence of an employment relationship is presumed between a person who performs a service and a person who receives the service, in return for payment or compensation. The FLL further establishes that an employment relationship means (regardless of the act from which it originates) the performance of work under the authority of another person, in return for compensation. In view of the above, the existence of a subordinate relationship will determine the real nature of the relationship between the individuals rendering the services and the beneficiary, regardless of any contract between the parties.

8.2.3. Compensation

Since labour rights may not be waived by employees, even if a commercial-type agreement is executed between the company and the individual, if the nature of the agreement is, in essence, an employment relationship, then the commercial agreement will be considered null and void. This will leave the independent contractor with the right to claim all the labour rights under the FLL, such as severance pay, vacation time, vacation premium, Christmas bonus, social security contributions owed to the IMSS, contributions to the INFONAVIT, and contributions to the National Retirement Fund (*Sistema de Ahorro para el Retiro (SAR)*), among others.

A special analysis is needed regarding the possible consequences and liabilities pertaining to the Mexican Social Security Institute and the tax authorities. The SSL states that it is mandatory to register employees with the IMSS and the INFONAVIT, whether they are full or part-time employees, and regardless of how the relationship originated or the legal structure or business of the employer, even when the latter, by law, may be exempt from the payment of taxes or duties.

Moreover, social security contributions are considered taxes, pursuant to the Federal Tax Code, and the IMSS has the authority to require payment of all social security dues an employer has not made. In addition to requiring such payment, the IMSS is entitled to assess inflation adjustments and fines. Finally, failure to pay these dues could be considered tax fraud and the employer would then be liable for the penalties set out in the Federal Tax Code.

8.2.4. Other Terms and Conditions

Not applicable.

8.3. CONTRACT WORKERS

The FLL allows fixed term and determined tasks employment agreements if the temporary nature of the services is fully substantiated. However, these atypical relations are only allowed as exceptions.

8.4. LEASED WORKERS

On 23 April 2021, it was published in the Official Gazette a reform of the FLL to prohibit *the practice of labour subcontracting, better known as* 'outsourcing' and 'insourcing', eliminating intermediation and Article 15-A, 15-B, 15-C and 15-D of the FLL regarding outsourcing, and adjusting the social security and tax legislation to this modification. However, the text of the reform establishes that the provision of specialized services or the provision of specialized works that are not part of the corporate purpose or the economic activity of the beneficiary company of the services will not be prohibited. Furthermore, the reform mandates that all providers of specialized services or specialized works must file before the Ministry of Labour an application to be included in a General Registry of providers and to be authorized to render those specialized services or works. The authorization of the Department of Labour is a mandatory requirement to provide those services, which must be formalized through a written agreement. The contracting party must obtain from the specialized services provider certain information to evidence that the provider has honoured its labour, social security and tax obligations. If all the requirements are not met, the contracting party will not be able to deduct the payments made to the provider for income tax purposes and will not be able to credit the value added tax. Likewise, the use of outsourcing schemes not allowed by the law or the simulation of any act to avoid the application of legal provision can be deemed as organized crime and the authority can impose fines and sanctions, including imprisonment.

8.5. CHECKLIST OF DOS AND DON'TS

– Do not execute independent contractor agreements when the real nature of the services to be provided call for an employment agreement.

- Do analyse whether the services to be provided will be subordinated to the company.
- Do perform due diligence on outsourcing companies before executing an agreement with them to ensure they comply with labour, tax and social security obligations.
- Do verify that the outsourcing company has its own and sufficient resources in order for the customer not to be considered as an employer of employees of the outsourcing company.
- Do outsource only specialized services.
- Do not outsource employees who will perform equal or similar activities than those employees directly hired.

9. OBLIGATION TO BARGAIN COLLECTIVELY WITH TRADE UNIONS: EMPLOYEES' RIGHT TO STRIKE AND A COMPANY'S RIGHT TO CONTINUE BUSINESS OPERATIONS

9.1. Overview of Unions' Right to Organize

According to the Mexican Constitution, all people located within the Mexican territory, including foreign individuals, are granted the right to organize and associate, as well as the freedom of expression.

Article 9 of the Mexican Constitution guarantees the right to peacefully assemble or associate for a legal purpose. The right to associate involves the creation of an entity with a different and independent capacity, and with a common purpose or objective that will transcend the course of time.

Furthermore, Article 123 specifically regulates the freedom of employees and employers to associate in defence of their common interests through unions and/or professional associations. This constitutes a social right granted to both employees and employers which, due to its nature, has to be exercised collectively.

The FLL defines a union as an association of workers or employees, which is constituted for the study, improvement and defence of their common interests. According to Article 364 of the FLL, in order to form a union, at least twenty active workers must associate with such purpose. The workers do not necessarily have to work in the same company or for the same employer.

On 1 May 2019, an important reform to FLL was published in the Official Gazette to modify labour provisions. Mexico was part of several international free trade agreements (Transpacific Partnership Agreement and United States, Mexico and Canada Agreement 'USMCA', the new North Atlantic Free Trade Agreement 'NAFTA') and, as a requirement from other countries, Mexico had to guarantee the freedom of association and the right of collective bargaining set forth by International Labour Organisation's Conventions 87 and 98. This is probably the most important reform since the law was enacted and will change the way companies do business in Mexico.

9.2. RIGHT OF EMPLOYEES TO JOIN UNIONS

The FLL clearly states that neither the employees nor the employers require any previous authorization to form a union; therefore, they are totally free to decide whether or not to join an existing union or to form a new one. However, employees under 15 years of age cannot join a union, and confidential employees are not allowed to join the same union as the rest of the employees.

According to Article 358 of the FLL no one can be obliged either to join a union or abstain from doing so, and any agreement or clause that contravenes this provision will be considered void. As we mentioned, on 1 May 2019, an important amendment to the FLL was published in the Official Gazette in order to guarantee the freedom of association. The right included in Article 358 was strengthened in order to make it clear that no one can be obliged to join a union and to guarantee the freedom of association, which includes three different aspects: (i) right to join a union; (ii) right to remain in that union, and (iii) right to not being unionized. Therefore, for the first time in Mexico, union-free environments are possible in Mexico.

Although, generally speaking, all employees have freedom of association, and therefore are entitled to join any union, the FLL allows CBA to establish a 'closed shop' *clause* providing that the employer may admit as employees only individuals who are members of the trade union that is a party to the agreement. This provision was not eliminated in the last reform.

9.3. HOW EMPLOYEES SELECT UNIONS

According to Article 360 of the FLL, employee unions may be: (a) guilds ('gremiales') composed of workers of the same profession, occupation or speciality; (b) a company union, composed of workers that render their services to the same company; (c) industrial unions, composed of workers that render their services to one or more companies in the same industrial field; (d) national industries, composed of employees that render their services to one or more companies in the same industrial field in two or more states; or (e) unions of various occupations, integrated by workers of different professions.

Furthermore, according to Article 361 of the FLL, employer unions can be: (a) composed of employers in one or more fields, or (b) composed of employers in one or more fields in different states.

Notwithstanding the above-mentioned categorization, there is almost no regulation regarding how employees decide which union to join.

9.4. PRE-ELECTION CAMPAIGNING

Mexican law provides that all elections or campaigns of labour unions must respect the right of freedom of association and must be carried out by direct, free, personal and secret vote. Unions must establish their own rules and procedures in their by-laws following these principles and they have one year after 1 May 2019 to modify their by-laws to establish these procedures.

It is not a common practice for the candidates to conduct pre-election campaigns.

9.5. UNFAIR LABOUR PRACTICES

Unfair labour practices are generally forbidden by the Constitution and by the FLL which includes special protection to working minors and pregnant women. One unfair labour practice that is specifically prohibited is the so-called blacklists (*listas negras*), which are lists of workers that were fired by one or more employers. It is therefore forbidden for employers to include the names of employees in a special list whose sole purpose is to prevent other potential employers from offering them a job.

9.6. RELOCATION OF WORK/SHUTDOWN OF BUSINESS

Employment relationships in Mexico are bilateral, and therefore it is not possible for the employer to unilaterally change any of the existing labour conditions, such as salary, position and place of work, without the written consent of the employee.

Any modification that implies a unilateral change of the employees' working conditions entitles such employee to file a complaint about constructive dismissal. In case of constructive dismissal, the company would have to pay severance according to the FLL (*see* section 4.2 above).

According to the foregoing, if an employer relocates the workplace, he/she needs to enter into modification agreements with the employees in order to establish the new address where the employees will have to render their services. It is also important to note that depending upon the distance between one workplace and the other or the employee's address and the workplace, the employer could be obliged to pay transportation expenses.

Regarding company shutdowns and collective redundancies, *see* sections 6.1 and 6.2 above.

9.7. CHECKLIST OF DOS AND DON'TS

– Do respect the union's right to organize.
– Do not disrupt the right of employees to join unions.
– Do negotiate with unions to prevent a strike.
– Do not use blacklists.

10. WORKING CONDITIONS: HOURS OF WORK AND PAYMENT OF WAGES: BY STATUTE OR COLLECTIVE AGREEMENTS

10.1. OVERVIEW OF WAGE AND HOURS LAWS

The FLL establishes minimum wages and limits on working hours. There is a minimum daily wage, which in some cases depends on the employee's occupation; however, it does not change due to age or experience.

The FLL establishes as a maximum weekly work shift the following:

– Eight hours per day shift (equivalent to forty-eight hours per week).
– Seven hours per night shift (equivalent to forty-two hours per week).
– Seven-and-a-half hours per mixed shift –part day and part night – (equivalent to forty-five hours per week).

10.2. MINIMUM WAGE

The minimum daily wage is determined every year by an administrative employer–employee–government organization (National Minimum Wage Commission) (*Comisión Nacional de los Salarios Mínimos (CONASAMI)*). On 30 September 2015, the National Minimum Wage Commission resolved that for effects of the application of the minimum daily wage in the Mexican territory, there would be one sole geographical area since 1 October 2015.

However, for 2019, CONASAMI established the country would be divided into two different zones: the Border Free Zone and the rest of the country. For 2021, the minimum daily wage for the Border Free Zone is MXN 213.39 (around USD 10.62) and for the rest of the country is MXN 141.70 (around USD 7.055).

In January 2021, the National Institute of Statistics and Geography (*Instituto Nacional de Estadística, Geografía e Informática (INEGI)*) announced the new value of the Unit of Measure and Update (*Unidad de Medida y Actualización (UMA)*) that will rule from 1 January 2021 to 1 January 2022: the daily value will be MXN 89.62, MXN 2,724.45 monthly, and MXN 32,693.40 annually.

INEGI's determination results from the constitutional reforms on de-indexation of the minimum wage which entered into force on 28 January 2016 and pursuant to which said wage ceased to be unit of account, index, base, measure or reference to determine the amount of the obligations and hypothesis established in federal and local laws, as well as any other legal provisions arising therefrom. Such is the case of Title Sixteen of the Federal Labour Law, which takes the general minimum wage as the basis for the calculation of fines deriving from violations of labour standards.

The Federal Congress, the local congresses, the Legislative Assembly of Mexico City, as well as the Federal, State and Municipal Public Administrations must have performed the corresponding adjustments to laws and ordinances within their competence for the effect of eliminating references to the minimum wage no later than 28 January 2017. However, according to Transitory Section Third of the Decree on De-indexation of the minimum wage establishes that from its entrance into force, all references to the minimum wage as unit of account, index, base, measure or reference to determine the amount of the obligations and hypothesis established in federal and local laws, as well as any other legal provisions arising therefrom must be understood as references to the UMA.

10.3. OVERTIME

An employee can only be required to work overtime in exceptional circumstances. Any employee who works more than the maximum total hours mentioned in section 10.1 above is entitled to:

- for the first nine extra hours per week, a payment of 200% of such hours; and
- for any additional hours exceeding those nine hours per week, the employee shall receive 300% of the payment for each exceeding hour.

The FLL provides for no more than three hours per day and three times per week of overtime (3 hours × 3 days = 9 hours a week). According to a binding opinion issued by the Supreme Court of Justice, overtime must be calculated and paid on a weekly basis.

Moreover, the Supreme Court of Justice issued another binding opinion according to which the minutes or fraction of an hour worked in addition to the ordinary work journey shall be accrued and paid per complete unit of hour.

Section XI of Article 123 of the Constitution limits overtime to three hours per day and provides that it may not be performed on more than three consecutive days; however, an employee may work as long as he/she consents to them and receives the corresponding pay as explained before.

10.4. MEAL AND REST PERIODS

In terms of the FLL, all employees must have a break of at least thirty minutes per shift to rest and have their meals. If employees are not allowed to leave the employer's facilities during such break, this time will be computed as time actually worked for work shift purposes.

The Supreme Court of Justice recently issued a binding opinion according to which, in order for the work day to be considered as discontinuous, the meal and rest period should last one hour at least, and the employee must be able to leave the company's premises. Otherwise, such a meal and rest period will be deemed as part of the work day.

The meal and rest periods could be extended through negotiation in the CBA or individual employment agreements.

10.5. DEDUCTIONS FROM WAGES

Article 110 of the FLL establishes that, other than the corresponding deductions for taxes or social security contributions, it is unlawful to make any deduction from employee salaries, except in the following cases and subject to the following conditions:

(1) Any overpayment made to the employee by the employer, such as an advance in wages, loans, errors, losses, or the purchasing of any articles produced by the company may be legally deducted from an employee's wages.
(2) The amount to be deducted shall in no way exceed one month's salary.
(3) The instalments and amounts deducted shall be agreed upon by both parties in writing.
(4) The 30% of the amount by which the employee's wage exceeds the minimum wage; that is to say, from the total monthly salary of the employee, the minimum wage shall be deducted (employee's monthly salary − minimum wage), then the employer may only deduct the 30% each month from the employee's salary until the employee pays back

the total debt, which again, cannot exceed one month of the employee's salary.

Regarding union dues, the 1 May amendment included the right of the worker to decide if he/she pays or not the union dues; therefore, now workers can express their will for not paying union dues.

10.6. GARNISHMENT

Although Article 112 of the FLL states that employees' salaries may not be garnished, except for legally mandated alimony and child-support payments, a recent resolution of the Supreme Court has determined that it is possible to garnish employees' salary subject to certain limitations.

10.7. EXEMPTIONS TO WAGE AND HOUR LAWS

In Mexico, there are no exemptions to wage and hour laws. All employees, regardless of their position, are entitled to receive overtime payments, as labour rights cannot be waived or contracted out by employees.

In March 2017, Second Chamber of the Supreme Court of Justice issued a binding opinion according to which if during a trial there is controversy regarding the length of the ordinary work journey and, indirectly, on the extraordinary work journey of an upper-level trustworthy employee holding the position of Director, Administrator or Manager, given the minimum possibility that the employer generates attendance controls for such employees, the burden of proof is on the employee because the employer is not in a better position to accredit such fact.

10.8. CHILD LABOUR

Under the Constitution, it is generally forbidden to employ children under 15 years of age; minors between 15 and 18 years of age who have not completed their compulsory education are not allowed to work. In order to work, children between 15 and 16 years of age require authorization from their parents or guardian, or failing this, from the trade union they belong to. Alternatively, the Conciliation and Arbitration Board or an inspector of the Labour Department can give the required authorization.

Furthermore, minors under 18 years are not allowed to work overtime.

It is also forbidden for children under 18 years of age to render services outside the Mexican Republic unless they are technicians, professionals, artists, athletes, or specialized workers.

The daily work shift for children under 16 years of age cannot exceed six hours, should be allocated in periods of three hours maximum and cannot be rendered after 22:00 hours.

Children under 18 years of age are also entitled to an annual vacation period of at least eighteen paid days.

Mexico, as a member of the International Labour Organization (ILO), has ratified several conventions, one of them being Convention Number 182 on the abolition of child labour.

10.9. Recordkeeping Requirements

10.9.1. Information That Must Be Maintained

Article 804 of the FLL establishes that the employer must keep the following documents in the employee's dossiers:

(a) Individual employment agreements.
(b) Payroll list and salary payment receipts.
(c) Work shift and attendance records.
(d) Fringe benefits payment receipts (profit-sharing, vacation, vacation premium, Sunday premium, Christmas bonus, overtime, bonuses, incentives and sales commissions).

In addition, there are other documents that are recommended to be kept in the employee's personal files:

– Employment application.
– Medical records.
– Recommendation letters.
– Employee's personal information.
– Performance evaluations.
– Vacation application and records.
– Life and medical insurance (if these benefits are provided).
– Any other benefits or agreement executed with the employee.
– Policies, shop rules or regulations acknowledgment forms, if any.
– Training records.
– Employee's registration and salary modification records filed with the IMSS.
– In case of employment termination, the written termination notice, resignation letter, termination agreement and/or full payment receipts.

– Data privacy notice.

In case of litigation, the employer has the burden of proof regarding the terms and conditions of employment. Therefore, all records should be kept until the litigation has ended or the statute of limitation expires, even if the terms therein described have elapsed.

10.9.2. Records That Must Be Retained

The time during which the employer is required to keep employee records depends on the type of document, as follows:

(a) Individual employment contracts should be kept during the entire time the employment relationship persists and one year after it has been terminated.
(b) Payroll lists, salary and fringe benefits payment receipts, work shift and attendance records should be kept for one year after the employment relationship is terminated.
(c) Pursuant to the SSL, the social security authorities have the right to claim outstanding social security dues for five years from the date on which the respective payment must have been made. Due to the foregoing, it is recommended to keep the following documents for at least five years:
 – payments to the Mexican Social Security Institute;
 – updated documents related to changes in the initial employee's information provided to the IMSS;
 – employee death, sickness and/or injury records.

10.9.3. Failure to Maintain Required Records

If, in case of litigation, the employer fails to provide the above-mentioned records, the allegations made by the employee will be presumed as true, unless otherwise proven.

10.10. REDUCTIONS IN COMPENSATION CAUSED BY ECONOMIC DOWNTOWN

As mentioned before, employment relationships are bilateral, and therefore it is not possible for the employer to change compensation without the written consent of the employee.

Indeed, any modification that implies a unilateral change of the employee's working conditions entitles such employee to file a complaint about constructive dismissal. In this regard, Article 51 of the FLL expressly establishes that the employee can file a complaint about constructive dismissal if the employer reduces the employee's salary. In case of constructive dismissal, the company would have to pay severance according to the FLL (*see* section 4.2).

An employer can execute a modification agreement with employees to authorize the reduction of salary and/or benefits. The modification agreement has to be ratified with the Conciliation and Arbitration Board and, if applicable, before the Conciliation Centre or Court to avoid any potential liabilities, in accordance with Article 33 of the FLL.

10.11. CHECKLIST OF DOS AND DON'TS

- Pay at least the minimum daily wage to employees, pursuant to the respective geographic area.
- Do not exceed the maximum daily work shifts or the maximum hours of overtime.
- Do pay overtime as provided by law.
- Do give employees a break of at least thirty minutes to rest and have meals.
- Do not make deductions from wages, except those specifically allowed by law.
- Do not garnish an employee salary, except as mandated by the authorities for alimony.
- Do maintain those employee documents required by law or recommended to be kept.
- Do not reduce an employee's salary and/or benefits without first obtaining his/her consent through a modification agreement.

11. OTHER WORKING CONDITIONS AND BENEFITS: BY STATUTE, COLLECTIVE AGREEMENTS, OR COMPANY POLICY

11.1. HEALTH AND OTHER INSURANCE

All employees must be registered with the IMSS. Once an employer has registered its employees with the IMSS, the employer is subrogated by the IMSS in all benefits, economic and in kind, which means that the IMSS will be responsible for the medical services for the employee and paying for the corresponding disability.

All employees must contribute to the IMSS, which provides medical services, child day care, compensation for occupational accidents and diseases, pensions upon death or disability, and pregnancy benefits.

Additionally, the employer may choose to provide additional health coverage through a private health insurance service. However, these employees must also be duly registered with the IMSS.

11.2. PENSION AND RETIREMENT BENEFITS

All employees must be registered with and contribute to the SAR, which provides employees with retirement benefits when they reach 65 years of age.

Pension contributions must be paid to the IMSS as follows:

- The employer pays 2% of the employee's base salary as pension contributions for retirement.
- The employer pays 3.15% of the employee's base salary as pension contributions for early retirement.
- Employees pay 1.125% of their base salary as pension contributions for early retirement.

Before 1997, the IMSS itself provided pensions to employees. As a result, employees who began working for their current employer prior to 1997 may still receive a pension from the IMSS.

Employees who began working for their current employer after 1997 can purchase an annuity payable for life from an insurance company when they reach the legal retirement age and receive a pension. This age is 60 for women and 65 for men, provided that at least 1,250 weeks of pension contributions have been paid to the IMSS.[5]

11.3. VACATION AND HOLIDAY PAYMENTS ON TERMINATION

Article 76 of the FLL states that employees with more than one year of services are entitled to at least six days of paid vacation leave per year. This increases by two days for each subsequent year of service, up to fourteen days. After the fourth year of service, vacation days increase by two for every five years of service.

---

5. SSL, Art. 162.

In addition to vacation pay, employees are entitled to an extra bonus of 25% of their base salary as a vacation premium.

Employees must use their vacation days, as it is against the law to pay the employee in exchange for those vacation days while the employee is still employed. Rights derived from labour relationships have a statute of limitations of one year for the employee to exert them; however, in the particular case of vacations, after the first year of services ends, an employer is entitled to six months to determine the vacation period. It is until after said six-month period expires that the employee is entitled to demand his vacation period under the one-year statute of limitations. Moreover, upon termination, the employee shall receive the payment of any outstanding vacation not used.

In addition, there are seven paid public holidays each year, and 1 December is a public holiday every six years when a new president is elected. Federal or state election laws may also grant a public holiday for regular elections.

It is also customary, but not mandatory, to give employees Thursday and Good Friday of the Easter week off as an additional paid holiday.

11.4. Leaves of Absence

11.4.1. Personal Leave

Employees could ask for unpaid personal leaves; however, the employer is not obligated to grant this type of leave of absence.

11.4.2. Medical or Sick Leave

An employee is entitled to sick leave, depending on the type of illness and degree of disability. In case of illness or injury, an employee must obtain a doctor's order from the IMSS. The IMSS determines the employee's entitlement to sick leave as well as the amount paid to the employee during the illness or injury. The IMSS, not the employer, pays the employee's income during the leave.

There is no mandatory unpaid medical leave of absence in Mexico. If the employee needs an unpaid medical leave of absence due to a condition not recognized by the IMSS, then the employer has the discretion to grant the leave.

11.4.3. Bereavement Leave

There is no mandatory bereavement leave; however, CBA usually establishes a paid leave in case of death of a close relative.

11.4.4. Family Leave

In Mexico, male employees are entitled to enjoy paternity paid leave of five days when the child is born or in case of adoption as of the placement of the child.

11.4.5. Pregnancy Leave

Working mothers are entitled to forty-two days prior to childbirth as pregnancy leave, and the IMSS pays them 100% of their registered salary during such leave. Moreover, working mothers may request to the employer the transfer of up to four weeks before the childbirth in order to enjoy them after childbirth.

11.4.6. Maternity Leave

Working mothers are also entitled to forty-two days after childbirth as maternity leave, with the IMSS paying them 100% of their registered salary.

Statutory maternity leave may be extended as necessary if work is not possible because of the pregnancy or the delivery. During the maternity leave, the employee receives her regular salary.

During the nursing period of six months, the new mother is entitled to two additional thirty-minute rest periods per day to feed the child in an adequate and hygienic place set aside by the employer.[6]

When returning from maternity leave, the employee is entitled to reinstatement, provided that not more than one year has passed since the date of delivery.[7] Maternity leave is included in the length of service.[8]

11.4.7. Injury at Work

The FLL provides leave due to:

---
6. FLL, Art. 170.
7. FLL, Art. 170, para. VI.
8. FLL, Art. 170, para. VII.

(1) *Occupational Injuries*: defined as any accident or disease to which the employees are exposed in the course of their employment, or any consequences thereof.
(2) *Industrial Accident*: defined as any organic injury, functional disturbance (whether immediate or subsequent) or death, occurring suddenly in the course of the employment or in as a result thereof (i.e., the place where or the time when the accident occurs is related to the employment).
(3) *Occupational Diseases*: defined as any pathological condition arising out of the continued action of a cause that has its origin or motive in the employment or in the environment in which the employee is obliged to render his or her services.

The consequences of any of the injuries described above, and the term they may last, according to the SSL, are as follows:

Injury	Period of Leave
Temporary disability	52 weeks (which may be extended to an additional period of 52 weeks).
Permanent partial disability	Permanent leave. Payment is through the IMSS according to the amounts established in FLL.
Permanent total disability	Permanent leave. Payment is through the IMSS according to the amounts established by the FLL.

The economic benefits paid by the IMSS due to illness are based on 60% of the employee's registered salary,[9] and they are paid as of the fourth day of absence.

The SSL establishes the periods of leave, depending on the division of the compulsory social insurance plan:

Division	Period of Leave
Workers compensation insurance for job-related injury and illness	According to the above-mentioned outline.
Illness	1 day to 52 weeks.

---

9. Employee salaries to be registered with IMSS are limited to twenty-five times the minimum salary in force.

11.5. Checklist of Dos and Don'ts

- Do register all employees with the IMSS.
- Make all the corresponding social security and pension contributions.
- Do not pay employees in exchange for their vacation days unless the employment is being terminated, in which case the employer has to pay for outstanding vacation days.
- Do grant leaves of absence as stipulated by law or established in the CBA.

11.6. Telework

On 11 January 2021, came into effect a new amendment on the FLL, to regulate teleworking. According to this reform 'telework' will be considered a mechanism to carry out tasks remotely using the advantages of information and communication technologies. It can usually be done from the employee's home, but they can also alternate between office and home. The main considerations are:

- There is no immediate or direct supervision of the employer.
- The use of information and communication technologies is necessary.
- More than 40% of the working time is from the employee's home.
- If the telework is carried out occasionally or sporadically it will not be considered as such.
- Written working conditions are mandatory.
- It must be included in the CBA.
- It must be included in the Internal Regulations (Handbook).
- The employer must reimburse the proportional part of telecommunications and electricity to the employee.

The change from on-site to home-office must be voluntary and established in writing, except in cases of duly accredited force majeure. In any case, when a modification is made to the home-office modality, the parties will have the right of reversibility to the on-site modality, for which they will be able to agree on the mechanisms, processes and times necessary to make valid their will to return to such modality.

Furthermore, the special conditions regarding security and health for telework will be established by the Ministry of Labour and Social Welfare by the emission of an Official Norm, which ought to consider the ergonomic, psychologic factors and other risks that could cause adverse effects to health, mental and physical integrity of the teleworkers. The aforementioned norm must be published before 12 July 2020.

12. WORKER'S COMPENSATION

12.1. Overview

As mentioned in section 10.2, there is a daily minimum wage for the one sole existing geographical area of the country.

The FLL[10] establishes that the salaries of confidential employees must be paid on a bi-weekly basis, and the salary of blue-collar employees must be paid on a weekly basis. All salaries must be paid in Mexican Pesos. The parties can agree that the salary is to be paid in a foreign currency, but they must establish the exchange rate to be used to convert the agreed amount into Mexican Pesos.

Apart from their salary, there are mandatory bonuses and benefits to which all employees are entitled:

– *Profit-sharing:* Employees are entitled to a share in the company's profits, currently fixed at 10% of the company's pre-tax income.[11]
– *Vacation premium:* Employees are paid an extra 25% of their usual salary during their vacation.[12]
– *Christmas bonus:* Employers must give each employee the equivalent of fifteen days salary by 20th December of each year.[13]
– *Sunday premium:* Employees who render services on Sunday are entitled to a 25% premium over the salary payable for that day.[14]

12.2. Checklist of Dos and Don'ts

– Do not pay employees a lower compensation than the daily minimum wage for that area.
– Pay confidential employees on a bi-weekly basis.
– Pay blue-collar employees weekly.
– Pay employees the mandatory bonuses, being profit-sharing, vacation premium, Christmas bonus and Sunday premium, as the case may be.

---

10. FLL, Art. 88.
11. FLL, Art. 117.
12. FLL, Art. 80.
13. FLL, Art. 87.
14. FLL, Art. 70.

13. COMPANY'S OBLIGATION TO PROVIDE SAFE AND HEALTHY WORKPLACE

13.1. OVERVIEW OF SAFETY AND ENVIRONMENTAL LAWS AND REGULATIONS

Employers have various responsibilities in relation to their employees' health and safety, which are mostly set out in:

- the FLL;
- the Federal Workplace Regulations regarding Health and Safety; and
- specific rules (standards) established by the Department of Labour.

The IMSS assumes most employer responsibilities regarding health, once an employee is registered with the IMSS and social security contributions are paid.

The Hygiene and Safety Regulations establish the following obligations:

- the Employer–Employee Safety and Hygiene Committee has to prepare an annual job programme;
- keep monthly inspection certificates for a six-month period or annual report;
- conduct a study to determine the risk level of fire or explosion for each substance or material handled while on the job;
- keep certificates of training and teaching to prevent, protect from and extinguish fires;
- prepare and keep an emergency evacuation plan in case of fire;
- implement operation and safety procedures to avoid fire risks;
- keep a list of the type of fire equipment, including instructions on how to use and reload the equipment;
- have a certificate of brigade against fire;[15]
- highlight emergency exits within the facilities, adequate for handicapped persons working in the company;
- conduct a fire drill at least once a year; and
- keep a record and statistics of occupational injuries during the last year and certificate of notice to the safety commission.

13.2. REQUIREMENTS

The following activities and documents are required by the laws and regulations mentioned above regarding safety in the workplace:

---

15. A group of employees that undergo a series of seminars to become fire safety brigade in case of fire in the company.

- The employer must establish places to render the services according to reasonable safety and hygiene standards in order to prevent occupational risks and harm to its employees. Also, the employer must verify that the pollution limits established by authorities are not exceeded and, if required, modify its facilities to comply with authority orders.[16]
- Participation in the incorporation of the employer–employee committee of safety and hygiene.[17]
- Supply a first-aid kit.
- Inform labour authorities of any occupational risk.[18]
- Post within the company's facilities the safety and hygiene internal regulations and policies.[19]

13.3. RIGHTS OF EMPLOYEES

Employees have the right to perform their duties in a safe workplace. It is also the employee's right and obligation to form the *Employer–Employee Safety and Hygiene Committee* within each facility and to participate in the committee. Employees also have the right to refuse to perform dangerous work.

Article 134 of the FLL establishes that employees have the responsibility to abide by the preventive safety and hygiene measures established by the company or by the authorities to guarantee employee and workplace safety.

Employees are forbidden by Article 135 of the FLL to take any action that may compromise their safety or that of their co-workers or facilities.

Pregnant or nursing women may not work night shifts in industrial plants in hazardous environments, or after 10:00 p.m. in commercial or service establishments. They are also relieved from overtime work.

Pregnant or nursing women cannot work in any situation where the mother's or child's health may be endangered.

13.4. RIGHTS OF EMPLOYER

Employers also have the right and obligation to incorporate and participate in the *Employer–Employee Safety and Hygiene Committee.*

As per Article 47 of the FLL, the employer has the right to dismiss an employee without liability and without payment of severance: (i) in case the employee carelessly threatens workplace safety (*paragraph VII);* and (ii) if the employee fails to follow safety procedures (*paragraph XII).*

---

16. FLL, Art. 132, para. XVI.
17. FLL, Art. 509.
18. FLL, Art. 132, para. XVII.
19. FLL, Art. 132, para. XVIII.

According to Article 132(XVIII), it is the employer's obligation to publicize within company facilities the safety and hygiene procedures and regulations. The internal regulations of the workplace should also contain hygiene and safety measures to be followed during the performance of the jobs.

13.5. SPECIFIC STANDARDS

The Department of Labour establishes specific rules which apply to hygiene and safety issues in industries such as mining, health providers, agricultural, pharmaceuticals and manufacturing companies. Typically, these specific rules apply to personal safety equipment, noise and pollution levels, rules to handle chemical substances and training to manage and clean equipment, machinery and facilities.

13.6. INJURY OR ACCIDENT AT WORK

The FLL has catalogued and described the types of work-related injuries and the amounts to be paid as severance depending upon the level of the disability.[20]

Temporary disability is defined as the loss of abilities or capabilities that prevent a person from working for a limited period of time.[21]

Permanent partial disability is defined as the decline of a person's abilities or capabilities to perform his/her work.[22]

Permanent total disability is defined as the loss of a person's abilities or capabilities to perform his/her work for the rest of his/her life.[23]

Compensation is based on the employees' registered salary for social security purposes and is paid directly to the employees by the IMSS.

Should an employee suffer an accident or injury during work, the first step is to go to the IMSS; be that the emergency room services in the IMSS hospitals or the clinic. The IMSS then takes upon itself the responsibilities and processes that the employee has to go through in order to recover. Separately from the employee's recovery process and payments from the IMSS during this period, the IMSS makes an assessment on the risk of the employer's facilities and employees risk while on their jobs. In accordance with this determination from the IMSS, the risk premium that the employer must pay could be increased.

---

20. FLL Art. 513.
21. FLL Art. 478.
22. FLL Art. 479.
23. FLL Art. 480.

For more information, *see* section 11.4.7 injury at work.

13.7. WORKPLACE VIOLENCE

Under Article 47 of the FLL, cause for termination without liability for the employer includes: dishonest or violent behaviour of the employee while on the job; dishonest or violent behaviour against co-workers, disrupting work discipline; threatening, insulting, or abusing the employer or the employer's family or anyone at the workplace, unless provoked or acting in self-defence; and intentionally damaging the employer's property.

In addition, the FLL provides that an employee may be dismissed without liability for the employer if he/she incurs in bullying in the workplace.

Therefore, if the employee engages in one of these violent behaviours, the employer can terminate the employee with cause and without any liability. According to Article 51 of the FLL, the employer has the analogous duty to guarantee a safe workplace; failure to comply results in the termination of the employment relationship with no fault to the employee (constructive dismissal).

13.8. FINES AND PENALTIES

The non-observance of any laws, regulations and rules issued by the Department of Labour could be punished by the respective authorities with either a fine (from 250 to 5,000 times the daily UMA in effect, depending on the corresponding authority's determination) or another penalty, depending on the severity of the infraction. However, as hygiene and safety in the workplace are regulated by several different laws, there are numerous penalties that could be imposed.

13.9. CHECKLIST OF DOS AND DON'TS

– Comply with all Hygiene and Safety Regulations.
– Establish workplaces with reasonable safety and hygienic standards in order to prevent occupational risks.
– Participate in the establishment of an employer–employee committee regarding company safety and hygiene.
– Have stocked first-aid kits and inform labour authorities in case of any work-related risk.
– Post in the company's facilities the hygiene and safety internal regulations and policies.

– Do not disobey the specific standards of hygiene and safety.

14. IMMIGRATION, SECONDMENT AND FOREIGN ASSIGNMENT

14.1. Overview Laws Controlling Immigration

Immigration matters in Mexico are governed by the Immigration Law and its correlated regulations.

14.2. Recruiting, Screening and Hiring Process

For any employer, at least 90% of its employees must be Mexican nationals.[24] In addition, all technical and professional employees must be Mexican nationals, unless there are no Mexican nationals qualified in a particular specialized field, in which case the employer is allowed to temporarily employ technical and professional foreign nationals, but in a proportion not exceeding 10% of those working in the relevant field of specialization. Also, all physicians, railway employees and employees on a Mexican-flagged ship must be Mexican nationals. Mexican civil aviation crews must be Mexican by birth.

The recruiting, screening and hiring process is the same as for nationals, *see* section 3 above; however, foreign employees must have a valid work permit before being hired.

14.3. The Obligation of Employer to Enforce Immigration Laws

Companies hiring non-Mexican nationals or that issue a job offer to a non-Mexican national have to obtain an employer registration record from the National Immigration Institute when hiring foreign employees and provide the respective notices to register and discharge them, in accordance with Article 166 of the Regulations to the General Immigration Law.

14.4. Fines and Penalties

According to Article 164 of the Regulations to the Immigration Law, every foreigner needs prior authorization from the Department of the Internal

---

24. FLL, Art. 7.

Affairs to perform any activity different from the one previously authorized, unless they are entitled to a condition of stay obtained by virtue of a job offer.

Additionally, Article 166 of these Regulations establishes the obligation of the employers to file the application of the employer's registration before the National Immigration Institute and update it at least once a year with the registration and discharge of foreign employees, the annual tax return and any other change happening to the employer.

In case of a breach of this provision, Article 168 of the Regulations establishes that the competent authority shall solve and request the institute to start the corresponding immigration administrative process.

14.5. SECONDMENT/FOREIGN ASSIGNMENT

According to Article 123 of the Federal Constitution, the FLL protects every employee within Mexico, regardless of the nationality of the employer or employee, the place of execution of the labour agreement or payment of salary. Once an employment relationship exists, all the rights and obligations under the FLL automatically apply, regardless of how the agreement is characterized by the parties.

In virtue of the foregoing, if an expatriate renders his/her personal, subordinated services to a company in Mexican territory, pursuant to Article 20 of the FLL, a labour relationship exists between the expatriate and said company, regardless of the expatriate's nationality.

The hiring of expatriates or the sharing of employees, such as in a secondment agreement between a company in Mexico and a foreign company, requires careful planning in order to avoid creating future problems for both companies involved in the employment relationship.

There is the risk of expatriates being considered as having a dual employment relationship, or in other words, being employed by both the Mexican company and the non-Mexican company, either resulting from a secondment type arrangement under which a non-Mexican company lends an existing employee to a Mexican company or from the structuring of the payment of salary and benefits.

If such a dual employment relationship were found to exist, under Mexican law not only the Mexican company but also the non-Mexican company would be required to comply with the FLL and the SSL, and give to the expatriate all the benefits accorded under the Mexican employment legal framework, such as social security, and payment of severance.

14.6. CHECKLIST OF DOS AND DON'TS

- Do require work permits for all expatriates or foreign nationals working for the company.
- Respect the 90%– Mexican nationals' rule in the company's workforce.
- Do have Mexican technical and professional employees, unless there are no qualified Mexican nationals.
- Obtain the employer registration record from the National Immigration Institute when hiring non-Mexican employees or when issuing a job offer to a non-Mexican national.
- File the application of the employer's registration before the National Immigration Institute and update it at least once a year with the registration and discharge of foreign employees.

15. RESTRICTIVE COVENANTS AND PROTECTION OF TRADE SECRETS AND CONFIDENTIAL INFORMATION

15.1. OVERVIEW

The best way to protect theft of trade secrets and confidential information is to execute confidentiality and non-disclosure agreements with employees and to implement codes of conduct and confidentiality policies. Confidentiality agreements are necessary for criminal and civil law requirements that establish the holder's duty to take any and all actions necessary to maintain the confidential information as such.

The FLL establishes the employee's general obligation to keep their employers' trade secrets confidential.[25] Employers are entitled to terminate employees who disclose trade secrets or confidential information, with cause and without liability.[26]

15.2. THE LAW OF TRADE SECRETS

The Federal Law to Protect Industrial Property ('FLPIP') regulates the protection of trade secrets, which are defined as any information for industrial or commercial application, kept confidential by any individual or business entity in order to obtain or have a competitive or economic advantage over third parties in the performance of economic activities, and in respect of which said party has adopted means or systems sufficient to preserve confidentiality and restrict access thereto.

---

25. FLL, Art. 134(XIII).
26. FLL, Art. 47(IX).

The FLPIP will protect trade secrets, provided that the information is related to the nature, characteristics or purposes of the products, production methods or processes or distribution or trade forms of the products or services.

Under the FLPIP, a trade secret does not include information that is in the public domain or that is known to a technician, due to information previously available. It also does not include information that must be disclosed by operation of law or court order, unless that information is furnished to and held by a person as a trade secret in order to obtain licenses, permits, authorizations, registrations or any other acts of a government authority.

The protected information must be contained in documents, electronic or magnetic media, and optical disks, microfilms or other similar instruments, and clearly identified as 'confidential'.

15.3. RESTRICTIVE COVENANTS AND NON-COMPETE AGREEMENTS

In the strictest sense, non-compete agreements are void under Mexican law; specifically, under Article 5 of the Mexican Constitution which states that:

> The State shall not permit the execution of any contract, covenant, or agreement having as purpose the restriction, loss or irrevocable sacrifice of personal freedom, whether because of work, education or religious vows. Further, a person may not legally agree to their own banishment or exile, or temporarily or permanently waive their right to practice a given profession or industrial commercial pursuit.

However, non-competes, or restrictive covenants, or non-solicitations may be included in an employment agreement or in a separate agreement, and the non-performance of said provisions on the part of the employee could be grounds for justified termination provided such clauses or agreements are limited in time, geographical scope and consideration are paid in exchange. A non-solicitation provision states that if the employee solicits an employee, client or vendor during the employment relationship, he or she could be terminated with cause.

15.4. CHECKLIST OF DOS AND DON'TS

- Execute confidentiality and non-disclosure agreements with employees.
- Implement codes of conduct and confidentiality policies to protect trade secrets.

– Limit restrictive covenants in time geographical scope and agree and pay consideration in exchange.

16. PROTECTION OF WHISTLEBLOWING CLAIMS

16.1. Overview

There is no specific statutory protection for employees who alert or provide information about possible breaches of the law or good corporate governance policies.

16.2. Checklist of Dos and Don'ts

Not applicable.

17. DISCRIMINATION IN THE WORKPLACE

17.1. Overview of Anti-discrimination Laws

In Mexico, discrimination laws in labour matters are not extensively developed. The FLL states that no worker may be discriminated against on the grounds of race, nationality, gender, age, disability, religion, migratory condition, health, sexual orientation, religion, sexual preferences, political opinion or social status. Article 3 of the FLL establishes as a general principle, among other matters, that: 'any distinction made against employees based on race, nationality, sex, age, disability, religion, migratory condition, health, sexual orientation, religion, political affiliation or social status is strictly prohibited'. However, it also established that distinctions, exclusions and or preferences based on the particular qualifications demanded by a determined labour are not considered as discriminatory. Article 132(VI) further requires employers to: 'treat employees with due consideration and avoid mistreatment by word or conduct', while Article 133(I) prohibits employers from: 'refusing employment (to an applicant) based on age or gender'. Article 164 provides that: 'women have the same rights and obligations as men'.

Employers who violate any of the above-mentioned provisions shall be subject to a fine of 250 up to 5,000 days of the UMA in effect.

The Federal Law to Prevent and Eliminate Discrimination prohibits any discriminatory practice that infringes on the principle of equal opportunity.

The federal government's interpretation of this law must be consistent with international treaties on discrimination to which Mexico is a party.

Notwithstanding the above-stated laws and legal provisions; there are no stipulations with respect to concrete sanctions or legal actions, should the employer incur in discriminatory acts. Therefore, regardless of the existence, in the paper, of these laws and provisions, the lack of enforcement thereof represents a standstill in the evolution of non-discriminatory legislation in Mexico.

17.2. AGE DISCRIMINATION

The FLL protects minors by establishing the following prohibitions and requirements:

- Children under 15 years of age are not allowed to work.
- Children over 15 but under 18 years of age that have not finished their middle school education cannot work unless they obtain the respective authorization from labour authorities.
- Children over 15 but under 16 years of age need their parents' or guardians' authorization to work.
- Children under 18 years of age cannot render services outside the Mexican Republic except in the case of technicians, professionals, artists, athletes and specialized workers in general.
- Children under 18 years of age cannot render services during the evening shift in any industrial job.
- Children under 16 years of age cannot work after 10:00 p.m.; on dangerous, hazardous or risky activities; and they cannot work in facilities where alcoholic beverages of immediate consumption are sold.

17.3. RACE DISCRIMINATION

Mexican law is silent about this specific type of discrimination; it is treated as general discrimination. *See* section 17.1 above.

17.4. SEX DISCRIMINATION/SEXUAL HARASSMENT

The General Law for the Equity of Men and Women aims to regulate and guarantee gender equality. It sets up the guidelines and mechanisms for the fulfilment of equality in the public and private sector by encouraging women's empowerment.

The FLL, however, does not specifically regulate sex discrimination aside from general discrimination. *See* section 17.1 above.

The FLL provides the definition for harassment and sexual harassment on Article 3-BIS. Furthermore, it establishes that an employee may be dismissed without liability for the employer if he/she incurs sexual harassment in the workplace. Among the several prohibitions that the FLL impose on employer, is to allow or tolerate sexual harassment within the workplace. The breach of this provision may result in the imposition of a fine of 250 up to 5,000 times the daily UMA in effect.

Federal and state criminal codes have established harassment as an offence. Under the Criminal Code for the Federal District, it is an offence for any person to harass another person repeatedly for sexual purposes.

Furthermore, Article 1916 of the Federal Civil Code (FCC) states that a person must be indemnified in cash for 'moral damages' when he or she is affected in his or her feelings, affections, beliefs, honour, reputation, private life, shape and physical appearance, or in the consideration that others have of such person. Furthermore, the same provision assumes that moral damage exists when a person's freedom or physical or psychological integrity is violated or diminished. Despite this assumption, in practice, it is difficult to prove the essential elements of the action which causes moral damage, taking into consideration its subjectivity.

17.5. HANDICAP AND DISABILITY DISCRIMINATION

In August 2009, the General Law for Handicap People was published. This law states that those with a physical handicap have to be included in society on equal grounds. Nonetheless, the FLL does not provide anything specific regarding disability discrimination, except that it falls into the general discrimination prohibited by the FLL. *See* section 17.1 above.

Despite the above-mentioned, in order to promote equity and diversity within the workplace, the FLL establishes the obligation for employers with more than fifty employees to have appropriate facilities for the performance of the services of employees with disability.

17.6. NATIONAL ORIGIN DISCRIMINATION

There is nothing specific regarding this type of discrimination. *See* section 17.1 above.

17.7. Religious Discrimination

Mexican legislation is silent regarding religious discrimination. However, it falls into the general discrimination prohibited by the FLL. *See* section 17.1 above.

17.8. Military Status Discrimination

There is no protection against military status discrimination.

17.9. Pregnancy Discrimination

The FLL expressly prohibits employers from requesting women to present pregnancy certificates for their hiring, promotion and continuation of their labour relationship.[27] Also, the FLL expressly provides that an employer cannot dismiss a woman or force her to resign from her job due to her pregnancy.[28]

Therefore, employers must restrain from asking applicants if they are pregnant, and from requiring a pregnancy test as a condition of employment, in order to prevent any unwanted negative publicity.

Also, the FLL grants special protection to women who are pregnant or breastfeeding by establishing the following limitations:

– They cannot work night shifts in industrial plants that have a hazardous work environment.
– They cannot work after 10.00 p.m. in commercial or service establishments.
– They cannot work overtime.
– They cannot carry out any work that could endanger their health or that of their child. This includes work involving the use of considerable force (such as lifting or pushing) and standing for long periods of time.
– When returning from maternity leave, the employee is entitled to be reinstated, provided that not more than one year has passed since the date of childbirth.

Please note that the 1 May reform included a provision stating that, when the employer terminates the employment relationship of a pregnant woman due to a justified cause, the employer must keep her registration with the Social Security Institute up to six months after the birth of the child.

---

27. FLL Art. 133 (XIV).
28. FLL Art. 133 (XV).

17.10. Marital Status Discrimination

The FLL provides that an employer cannot dismiss a woman or force her to resign due to a change in her marital status.

17.11. Sexual Orientation Discrimination

Mexican legislation does not provide any specific regulation regarding sexual orientation discrimination; however, it also falls into the general discrimination prohibitions. *See* section 17.1 above.

17.12. Retaliation

The law does not prohibit retaliation; however, most companies include such a provision in their compliance programmes and policies.

17.13. Constructive Discharge

Article 51 of the FLL regulates constructive dismissal and establishes several causes for employment termination without any liability for the employee. However, these causes are not directly related to discrimination, except for the lack of probity or honesty.

17.14. Checklist of Dos and Don'ts

- Do not discriminate against workers on the grounds of race, gender, age, religion, political opinion, social status, migratory condition, health condition, marital status, disability or sexual orientation.
- Do not mistreat employees by word or conduct.
- Provide equal job opportunities for men and women.
- Do provide equal job opportunities to people within the legal working age.
- Do not employ children without complying with all legal requirements.
- Do not ever allow sexual harassment in the workplace.
- Do not discriminate against disabled persons.
- Do not require pregnancy tests or refuse employment to pregnant women.
- Do comply with work restrictions regarding pregnant women.
- Do provide appropriate facilities for the performance of the services of employees with disability.

18. SMOKING IN THE WORKPLACE

18.1. Overview

Recently, a non-smoking culture has started to develop from a legal standpoint, as the culture on human rights is in development in Mexico. Almost all international companies have internal regulations, policies and procedures (soft law) that restrict or prohibit smoking.

On 30 May 2008, the General Law for the Control of Tobacco was published. This law forbids smoking in closed public places, which for the benefit of the common benefit, must be 100% smoke-free. Internal working areas, either public or private, must have specific smoking areas which have to be outside. Employers have an obligation to enforce these non-smoking regulations and internal policies of the company.

18.2. Checklist of Dos and Don'ts

- Comply with legislation regulating tobacco consumption by either maintaining the workplace 100% smoke-free or designate specific open areas for smoking.
- Do include smoking policies in the internal regulations and codes of conduct.
- Enforce non-smoking laws and policies in the workplace.

19. USE OF DRUGS AND ALCOHOL IN THE WORKPLACE

19.1. Overview

Reporting to work under the influence of alcohol or non-prescription drugs is considered a cause for termination without liability to the employer, as provided by Article 47(XIII) of the FLL. However, in order to evidence the above in case of litigation, the employer needs a doctor's order stating that the employee was under the influence of alcohol or drugs while he was in the workplace.

The employer needs the employee's consent to obtain the doctor's order. Therefore it is advisable to include either in the individual employment agreement, the CBA or in the internal regulations of the company that employees shall submit to periodical medical examinations during their employment with the company, so as to prevent any employee from refusing to undergo any examination, or to include such refusal among the causes for termination of the employment.

19.2. CHECKLIST OF DOS AND DON'TS

- Include in the individual or collective agreement or internal regulations that employees shall submit to periodical medical examinations.
- Obtain a doctor's order in case the employee reports to work under the influence of alcohol or drugs.
- Do not try to dismiss an employee with cause without any medical evidence that he/she was under the influence of alcohol or drugs while at work.

20. AIDS, HIV, SARS, BLOOD-BORNE PATHOGENS

20.1. OVERVIEW

In Mexico, laws that deal with sick, HIV employees or employees with AIDS are not fully developed yet. There are some laws, such as the Federal Law to Prevent and Eliminate Discrimination, official recommendations issued by the Human Rights Commission and International Agreements issued by the ILO and ratified by Mexico, which establish that HIV employees have the same right to get and maintain their job and receive training as any other employee, and that they shall not be discriminated against as a consequence of their condition.

All regulations and recommendations rest in local legislation, such as in Mexico City, to establish any special protection to individuals who need it, for any reason such as sexual orientation, gender, age and/or disability.

There is no enforceable prohibition (with direct actions against the employer) on terminating HIV-positive employees or employees with AIDS. However, employees have commenced negative public and media campaigns against employers who dismiss them because of their condition.

20.2. CHECKLIST OF DOS AND DON'TS

- Do not disclose an employee's sickness since medical records must be kept confidential.
- Do not discriminate against employees with these kinds of illnesses.
- Do promote non-discrimination practices in the workplace.

21. DRESS AND GROOMING REQUIREMENTS

21.1. Overview

There is no regulation regarding dress and grooming in the workplace; however, the employer can establish dress codes and grooming policies in the company's ILR, codes of conduct or dress codes.

21.2. Checklist of Dos and Don'ts

– Do regulate employee dress and grooming in the company's internal regulations, code of conducts and dress codes.

22. PRIVACY, TECHNOLOGY AND TRANSFER OF PERSONAL DATA

22.1. Privacy Rights of Employees

With regard to the protection of the employees' personal information, the FLPPD, published on 5 July 2010 which took effect 6 July 2010, sets forth that all personal data processing (gathering, disclosure, storage, and use) is subject to the consent of the individual to whom such data belongs ('data subject'), unless such processing is contemplated within one of the exceptions provided by such law. Nevertheless, the FLPPD establishes that for the processing of financial and/or sensitive personal information, the data subject's consent must be expressly provided. The same requirements apply across the board, that is, in situations involving customers, etc., as well as in regard to employees.

In general terms, there are two main obligations under the FLPPD that must be observed by the data controller: (i) the need to deliver a privacy notice to the data subject, which must comply with specific requirements set forth below, and (ii) the creation of a personal data department, which will promote the protection of personal data within the private entity and represent the private entity if an application for access, rectification, cancellation or objection is filed with the data protection authority (Federal Institute for Access to Public Information and Data Protection).

The mandatory minimum requirements of the privacy notice are as follows:

(a) identity and address of the data controller;
(b) personal data to be processed;
(c) purposes of data processing;

(d) options and means offered by the data controller to limit the use or disclosure of personal data;
(e) means of exercising the rights to access, rectify, cancel or object to the subject's personal data processing;
(f) procedure to revoke the agreement for data processing;
(g) national and/or international transfers to be made (if any);
(h) if sensitive data will be processed;
(i) procedure and means whereby the data controller will notify the data subjects on changes to the privacy notice;
(j) information related to the company's data protection department or individual in charge of the treatment of personal information;
(k) options for the data owner to object to the data processing with respect to unnecessary purposes;
(l) provision on the use of tools allowing automatic and simultaneous gathering of data (such as cookies and web beacons).

In December 2011, the Regulations to the FLPPD were published and became effective. These regulations complement the obligations established in the FLPPD and provide specific guidelines regarding data protection throughout Mexico, security measures to protect personal data (which shall have been implemented within the following eighteen months to the effective date of the Regulations) and self-regulation mechanisms that could be implemented by the parties.

As both the FLPPD and its Regulations have become effective, the obligations imposed on the data controller are fully enforceable.

22.2. CHECKLIST OF DOS AND DON'TS

- Do draft privacy notices to be signed in original by employees.
- Do appoint a data controller within the company.
- Do not disclose personal information without the employee's consent.

23. WORKPLACE INVESTIGATIONS FOR COMPLAINTS OF DISCRIMINATION, HARASSMENT, FRAUD, THEFT, AND WHISTLEBLOWING

23.1. OVERVIEW

Investigation procedures are usually established in the company's policies or in the company's ILR.

Workplace investigations are generally very common, and employees must participate in such investigations conducted by the employer.

23.2. Checklist of Dos and Don'ts

– Do have ILR and policies updated and duly signed by employees.
– Do consider that in case of labour claim, the employer always has the burden of proof; therefore, the participation of experts is usually recommended, especially in fraud and theft investigations.
– Do have the company's policies updated and duly signed by employees.

24. AFFIRMATIVE ACTION/NON-DISCRIMINATION REQUIREMENTS

24.1. Overview

Mexican law does not contemplate affirmative action; nonetheless, it does regarding discrimination. *See* section 17 above.

24.2. Checklist of Dos and Don'ts

Not applicable.

25. RESOLUTION OF LABOUR, DISCRIMINATION AND EMPLOYMENT DISPUTES: LITIGATION, ARBITRATION, MEDIATION AND CONCILIATION

25.1. Internal Dispute Resolution Process

Companies could have internal dispute resolution processes; however, they are not mandatory, as the parties will always be entitled to raise their actions with the Conciliation and Arbitration Boards.

25.2. Mediation and Conciliation

There is no mediation and conciliation except for the formal conciliation process performed by the Conciliation and Arbitration Boards and, if applicable, Conciliation Centres.

25.3. ARBITRATION

Arbitration was always performed by the Conciliation and Arbitration Boards, as it is not possible for the parties to agree on a third-party arbitration; however, after the 2019 Labour Reform is totally in force, the Conciliation Centre will be the main authority to solve disputes. For a labour-related ruling to be enforceable, it must be issued by the competent labour authority.

25.4. LITIGATION

Conciliation and Arbitration Boards were the only administrative agencies in charge of solving labour disputes; nonetheless, after the Labour Reform is fully into force, the Conciliation Centres will become the main administrative body to solve disputes before litigation starts and labour courts will be the judicial body in charge of solving most legal disputes regarding labour law and its application. Up until today, when dealing with individual litigation cases (most of which are based on the employee's claim of an unfair dismissal/wrongful termination), a Board will encourage the parties to reach a settlement agreement before the actual proceedings take place.

If the parties refuse to reach an agreement, a Board will initiate the process; however, the parties may reach an agreement at any moment before the final award is issued.

According to the FLL, employees who have been wrongfully terminated can file a complaint with the Conciliation and Arbitration Board for: (a) constitutional severance consisting of three months of aggregate salary; or (b) reinstatement to the same position he/she held, plus back wages (which are the salaries the employee is not earning during the labour proceedings capped to one year, if the litigation is not concluded after twelve months, the plaintiff will be entitled to request 2% monthly interest over a fifteen-months' salary base).

Under Article 692 of the FLL, employees may be represented in the labour proceedings with a simple proxy letter signed by the employee along with two witnesses.

Upon the filing of an employee's claim, the Board will declare its jurisdiction and establish the time and date for the labour proceedings. The Board will serve process on the respective employer, and the proceedings will then take place.

The first hearing is divided into two stages. The first stage is the conciliation phase, mentioned above. In the second stage, the employee will ratify, modify or clarify his/her claim, and the employer will answer the complaint; subsequently, the employee and the employer will have the opportunity to refute each other's allegations. A second hearing shall be scheduled for the parties to present their evidence, and for each party to object to the evidence offered by the other party. Then the Board studies and decides which are admissible.

The employer always has the burden of proof, except under certain specific circumstances. For example, the employee has to prove that he/she has worked overtime or has worked on Sundays.

After all the evidence has been presented, the Board will issue a final ruling and depending on the result of the proceedings (which usually takes between eighteen months and two years), each party is entitled to a first appeal ('amparo' proceeding) with a federal judge. The federal judge's ruling can be appealed to the collegiate courts.

Please note that, as stated before, as part of the amendment to the FLL, the labour justice system was modified in order to eliminate Conciliation and Arbitration Boards to create new Conciliation Centres and labour courts, part of the judicial branch of the government. Likewise, the procedural rules were changed; however, due to budget issues, these modifications have only come into force in eight states, is starting in thirteen more this year (2021) and will be fully in force by the end of 2022.

25.5. FINES, PENALTIES AND DAMAGES

The Social and Welfare Department can impose fines of different amounts on employers.

In very specific cases when the employer has paid employees less than the general minimum daily salary or has issued payment receipts for amounts greater than those actually paid to employees, the employer can be sentenced to prison for three months to four years.

There are no damages allowed under the FLL; however, employees could claim *back wages*, which are the salaries the employee is not receiving from the termination date until and for a maximum of twelve months. Once the said period has concluded, a monthly interest rate of 2% will be generated on fifteen months of the employee's wage, which is to be paid once the process has concluded and in case the employer is found liable.

25.6. CHECKLIST OF DOS AND DON'TS

(1) Keep employee information and labour-related documents in anticipation of a potential labour dispute.

(2) Do have Powers of Attorney duly drafted and signed in order to represent the company in a labour dispute.
(3) Do accept notice of litigation labour dispute and appear at the proceedings, even when dealing with employees of third parties, to avoid a default case against the company.

26. EMPLOYER RECORDKEEPING, DATA PROTECTION, AND EMPLOYEE ACCESS TO PERSONNEL FILES AND RECORDS

26.1. OVERVIEW

The Data Privacy Law and its secondary regulations, among other laws, provide for the protection of personal information and rights to access, rectify, cancel and oppose its treatment by the private sector. The incorporation of such rights obeys current international tendencies and foresees the obligation of the responsible party to treat personal data of individuals, including employees and applicants on a confidential basis and for purposes informed to the holder of the data.

26.2. PERSONNEL FILES

Information contained in the employee's personnel file shall be kept confidential. *See* section 10.9 above for the documentation that should be kept in personnel files.

26.3. CONFIDENTIALITY RULES

Confidentiality rules may be implemented in handbooks, company policies and ILR. Employees have an obligation to follow them, and if they disclose any company confidential information, the employer would be entitled to terminate the employment relationship without any liability, as provided in Article 47(IX) of the FLL.

26.4. EMPLOYEE ACCESS

The employer is not obligated to allow employees access to personnel files and records but needs to grant access to personal data.

Medical files must be maintained discreetly and in confidence and must only be disclosed to third parties by means of a written order issued by the competent authorities, such as courts and health agencies. However, employees can request access to their own medical files, and the employer is required to grant such access.

27. REQUIRED NOTICES AND POSTINGS

27.1. OVERVIEW

The notices and postings required by law, and which the employer must disclose to employees, are the following:

(1) Termination Notice. An employer must give the employee written notice that clearly establishes the causes and date of termination; otherwise, the dismissal may be deemed unjustified regardless of the cause.
(2) The ILR. The FLL provides that the regulations will only be in force from the date of their filing with the Centre for Conciliation and Labour Registry; they must also be printed and distributed among the employees and placed in a visible site on company grounds. It is also advisable to keep a written acknowledgement form whereby employees recognize receiving and agreeing to abide by the Regulations.
(3) CBA. The FLL provides that the CBA have to be filed with the Centre for Conciliation and Labour Registry, and the complete text of the CBA has to be posted within the visible site of the workplace.
(4) Profit-Sharing Project. The Profit-Sharing Employer–Employee Committee shall post the profit-sharing plan within the company's facilities, for the employees to make comments and/or objections.
(5) Seniority Chart. The FLL specifies that employers must post on company grounds a chart containing the seniority of each employee; however, this is uncommon.

27.2. CHECKLIST OF DOS AND DON'TS

– Do deliver termination notices to employees, when employment is being terminated with cause.
– Do distribute the company's ILRs among the employees.
– Do place the company's ILRs and CBA visible places on company grounds.

– Do keep all the documents that prove the company's compliance with profit-sharing obligations.
– Have the employees acknowledge in writing that they received and agree to abide by the Regulations.

Updates

In April 2016, President Enrique Peña Nieto sent to the Senate a bill to substantially amend the Constitution on labour justice.

The bill proposed disappearing the Conciliation and Arbitration Labour Boards, which have been the agencies in charge of labour justice and their replacement by federal labour courts belonging to the federal judicial branch and by local labour courts belonging to the local judicial branch.

This initiative was discussed and approved by both the Senate and the Chamber of Representatives and was sent to the local congresses for their approval. The proposed constitutional reform was approved by seventeen local congresses. On 24 February 2017, the bill amending several provisions of sections 107 and 123 of the Mexican Constitution was published in the Official Gazette and became effective on 24 February 2018.

As a result of this constitutional reform, labour justice will be provided by labour courts belonging to the federal or local judicial branch, which will give them more independence in relation to the executive branches.

It is also relevant that with the constitutional reform a decentralized organism is created, independent of the federal administration and similar bodies in the States, which will be in charge, in the federal jurisdiction, of substantiating a mandatory pre-trial instance for the parties, which aims to fasten labour proceedings. Also, this organism will be in charge of the registration of union and CBAs.

This constitutional reform necessarily involves adjustments to the Regulatory Law, especially on procedural labour matters.

On 1 July 2018, Mexico had federal and local elections for several political positions, including the President, State Governors, Majors, among others.

Andrés Manuel López Obrador (AMLO), candidate of the National Regeneration Movement (MORENA, by its acronym in Spanish) won the Presidential election with 53% of the votes.

For the first time in Modern History, Mexico will be governed by a leftist President.

MORENA, which ideology is based on social equality and egalitarianism, also won the majority of both Chambers of the Congress.

The main points in MORENA's labour and employment agenda are:

- Young people – Empower young people by allowing them universal access to education and granting economic scholarships to all students.
- Minimum wage – Increasing the minimum daily wage (back then in MXN 88.36, approximately USD 4.65). This topic has been addressed during Trans-Pacific Partnership Agreement (TPP) and NAFTA's negotiations by the governments of the US and Canada.
- Outsourcing – This topic has been regulated by the Mexican tax and labour authorities during the last years to avoid violations to labour rights and tax fraud; therefore, MORENA has proposed to regulate even more this figure to guarantee labour rights to all employees.
- CBAs – There has been international pressure to abolish the practice of executing non-active CBAs. MORENA has proposed to ratify Convention 98 of the ILO to guarantee the right to collective bargaining, as well as to apply ILO Convention 87 regarding freedom of association.

During AMLO's administration, it is probable that there will be new Union Confederations, led by Napoleón Gómez Urrutia, leader of the Mining Union and who was exiled in Canada since 2006. He was registered as MORENA's elected Senator on 27 August 2018:

- Labour Ministry – AMLO has announced that Luisa María Alcalde will be appointed as Labour Secretary, who has proposed to implement the constitutional reform and the application of Conventions 87 and 98 of ILO.
- Amendment to the FLL – The reform has been approved and published by the Government on 1 May 2019.

The Reform implements the constitutional reform. Considering that MORENA won the majority of the Federal Congress, in charge of the preparation and approval of the FLL Bill, one can anticipate that the reform will include pro employees and unions provisions in order to create a better system.

Since the current President took Office, he has implemented a programme called Youth Constructing the Future. He also increased the general minimum wage from MXP 88.36 to MXN 141.70 and has created and passed a Labour Reform prohibiting the outsourcing of personnel. Finally, he indeed appointed Luisa Maria Alcalde as Labour Ministry.

On 6 June 2021, Mexico will be celebrating 'intermediate elections' in which certain Governors and the members of the House of Representatives; hence, these elections will establish whether or not MORENA keeps the majority such chamber.